GROS MORNE NATIONAL PARK

MICHAEL BURZYNSKI

Gros Morne
Co-operating Association

Parks
Canada
Parcs
Canada

BREAKWATER

BREAKWATER BOOKS LTD.
100 Water Street
P.O. Box 2188
St. John's, NF
A1C 6E6

Cover photo: Hiking in the Long Range Mountains. Michael Burzynski.
Maps and illustrations: Michael Burzynski
Editor: Heidi Cramm
Layout and design: John Andrews

Canadian Cataloguing in Publication Data
Burzynski, Michael, 1954-
Gros Morne National Park
ISBN 1-55081-135-5

1. Gros Morne National Park (Nfld.) -- Guidebooks. I. Title.
FC2164.G76B87 1999   917.1804   C97-950097-4
F1124.G76B87 1999

Published by Breakwater Books Ltd. in co-operation with the Gros Morne
Co-operating Association and Parks Canada

© Her Majesty the Queen in Right of Canada 1999
Photographs © Parks Canada unless otherwise noted.

Printed in Canada by Transcontinental Printing.

Canadä We acknowledge the financial support of the Government of
Canada through the Book Publishing Industry Development
Program (BPIDP) for our publishing activities

The publisher gratefully acknowledges the financial support of the Government of
Newfoundland and Labrador that has helped to make this publication possible.

TABLE OF CONTENTS

MAPS

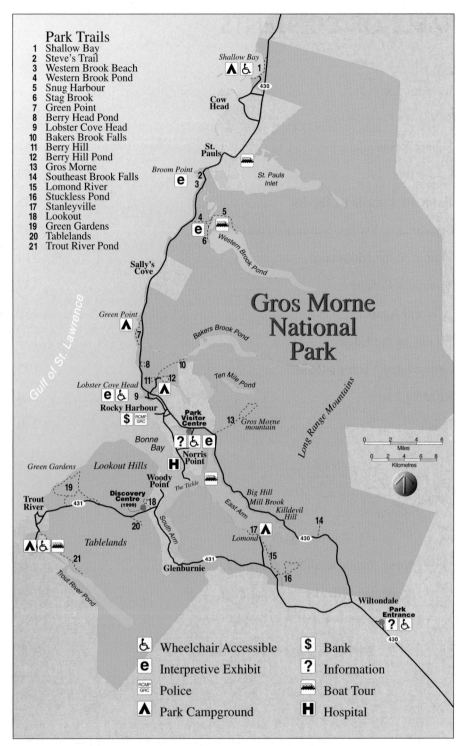

Park Trails

1 Shallow Bay
2 Steve's Trail
3 Western Brook Beach
4 Western Brook Pond
5 Snug Harbour
6 Stag Brook
7 Green Point
8 Berry Head Pond
9 Lobster Cove Head
10 Bakers Brook Falls
11 Berry Hill
12 Berry Hill Pond
13 Gros Morne
14 Southeast Brook Falls
15 Lomond River
16 Stuckless Pond
17 Stanleyville
18 Lookout
19 Green Gardens
20 Tablelands
21 Trout River Pond

Gros Morne National Park

☐ Wheelchair Accessible

e Interpretive Exhibit

RCMP/GRC Police

⚠ Park Campground

$ Bank

? Information

🚤 Boat Tour

H Hospital

Major facilities and trails of Gros Morne National Park.

PREFACE

ROS MORNE NATIONAL PARK HAS BEEN ON MY MIND for a long time. I started working with Parks Canada in 1973 as a summer naturalist at Fundy National Park in New Brunswick. Gros Morne was officially established that year, and I heard glowing descriptions of the park from friends who had visited or worked there. Two years later I made my first trip to Gros Morne, with my father and my brother John. We were shown around by a friend, Stephen Clayden, who was working in the park that year, and Gros Morne made a lasting impression on me. In 1978 I met Anne Marceau at Fundy, and since then we have worked together as naturalists and interpreters. We jumped when a chance arose to work in Gros Morne, a decision that we never have regretted.

Since arriving in Gros Morne in 1989, Anne and I have explored the park during hikes, ski and snowshoe trips, canoe and kayak paddles, photographic expeditions, and other outings with friends, relatives, and workmates. I would like to thank Bob Hicks, Sue Rendell, Brian Bonnell, Sheldon Stone, Geoff Hancock, Scott Taylor, Michael Murray, Todd Keith, Annette Luttermann, Sue Meades, Fred French, Julien Marceau, Chris Oravec and Jean Bédard for sharing adventures and misadventures off the beaten path; Rob Hingston, David Morrow, Clem Reid, Suzanne Barnes, Daniel Boisclair, Doug and Marilyn Anions, Lisa Paon, Danielle Richard, Fred Sheppard, Blake Maybank, George Case, and Daphne Porter for friendship at work and play; Hank and Joanne Deichmann for always keeping an open door; and Roger Smith, Michael Wood and Jamie Steeves for photographic inspiration. I am also grateful to the many other park staff, friends, and visitors whose observations and questions have helped me see this park more clearly.

I have had the pleasure of speaking to and taking field trips in the park with many researchers, including geologists Bob Stevens, Hank Williams, and Tony Berger; geomorphologist Doug Grant; geographer Ian Brookes; marine biologist Bob Hooper; botanists André Bouchard, Stuart Hay, and Luc Brouillet; archaeologists Charles Lindsay and Priscilla Renouf; wildlife biologist Shane Mahoney; and historian Jim Candow. I thank you for all your help.

Many local residents have helped me to understand this special place and I would like to express my appreciation to Amy Nicholle, Gord Shears, Ted Shears, Carl and Lovlet Rumbolt, Bill Bennett, Karole and Gary Pittman, Colleen Kennedy, Marilyn Parsons, Terry Organ, Stan and Jenny Parsons, and the late John and Elsie Harding.

Most of all, both Anne and I owe our love of the outdoors and our fascination with natural history to our parents Brenda and Toni Burzynski, and Margaret and Pat Marceau—many thanks for all those family drives in the country, hikes in the forest, mushroom- and berry-picking trips, fishing expeditions, and walks on the beach that started us down this path.

Gros Morne mountain has lent its name to the park.

INTRODUCTION

ROS MORNE IS A MOUNTAIN, AND THE MOST VISITED part of the Long Range highlands. It stands apart from the rest of the Long Range, but represents the climate, scenery, geology, and wildlife of the entire plateau. It is also the heart of a national park that bears its name.

The name is a reminder that until 1904 the French fished these shores. *Gros* means big, and *morne* is a Creole word for a rounded mountain standing apart from other hills. There are other Gros Mornes throughout the world: on Newfoundland's Baie Verte peninsula, on Québec's Gaspé peninsula, and on the islands of Martinique and Haiti. The top of Gros Morne mountain is literally the *Top of Gros Morne*—the highest point in the park, and short by only a few metres of the highest point on the Island of Newfoundland. *Morne* can also mean "dismal" or "gloomy," so although Gros Morne means "big isolated hill," when clouds rake across the mountaintop the gloomy description can seem very appropriate. Although somewhat redundant, the term *Gros Morne mountain* is used to differentiate between the hill and its namesake national park.

Gros Morne was established as a national park in 1973, and comprises 1,805 square kilometres of mountain and lowland, forest and bog, fjord and seashore. The park is a sample of the highlands and coastal lowlands of western Newfoundland Island—the physical regions that the park was established to represent. Like the mountain, Gros Morne National Park is set apart from its surroundings but remains inextricably tied to them.

Gros Morne is the largest national park in eastern Canada, but contains less than 0.5% of the land area of the province. However, Gros Morne has become the destination for more visitors than any other place on

Gros Morne mountain as seen from Woody Point.

James Steeves, GMNP

Newfoundland's west coast. Gros Morne is spectacular and wild, and contains examples of the habitats, scenery, and human history of this coast—but a visit to the park is only a glimpse at what can be seen to the north and south.

Gros Morne National Park received international recognition in 1987 when the United Nations Educational, Scientific, and Cultural Organization (UNESCO) declared it a World Heritage Site for its complex geology and remarkable scenery. Gros Morne joined the company of other World Heritage Sites such as Australia's Great Barrier Reef; Ecuador's Galapagos Archipelago; the Palace of Versailles in France; the pyramids from Giza to Dahshur in Egypt; Tikal National Park in Guatemala, Ngorongoro Conservation Area and Serengeti National Park in Tanzania; Canada's Nahanni National Park, Burgess Shale Fossil Site, and L'Anse aux Meadows National Historic Site; and Yellowstone, Redwood, and Olympic National Parks in the USA.

CANADA'S NATIONAL PARKS

As a national park, Gros Morne is a member of a country-wide system of terrestrial and marine protected areas. So far there are 38 national parks in Canada. Eventually a sample of each of Canada's natural regions—the major landscapes and seascapes of our country—will be preserved within a national park.

Trout River Pond and the Tablelands.

In 1936, Prime Minister Mackenzie King said of Canada that "...if some countries have too much history, so we have too much geography...." Sixty years ago it was possible to think of Canada's wild lands as endless, and man's effect on them as negligible. But today Canada, like the rest of the world, is rapidly running out of wild places.

Gros Morne and our other national parks are a treasure for us to guard and to enjoy. They must last forever—and may be one of our most important gifts to posterity.

THIS GUIDEBOOK

The first chapters explore the natural and human history of Gros Morne and its surroundings, and attempt to explain some of the most interesting aspects of this complex park. The last chapter contains suggested itineraries, information about accommodations and services, descriptions of hiking trails and ski trails, and other information to help visitors to the park.

KNOW YOUR LIMITS

Gros Morne National Park is a wilderness area. Wilderness has no railings, fences, or warning signs to keep you away from dangerous situations. *While in the park you are responsible for your own safety.* Avoid unnecessary risks.

You alone can assess your experience, your physical and mental limitations, and your abilities. Be sure of yourself before you embark on a trip—you will have a more pleasant time if you avoid situations beyond your ability. Wilderness travel (especially on the Long Range) is physically difficult, and life-threatening situations can arise. Be sure that your clothing, footwear, hiking and tenting equipment, and food supplies are adequate. If you plan to hike off-trail, be sure that you know how to use a map and compass before you leave. You cannot learn when you are lost.

We try to ensure that descriptions of trails and traverses are as accurate as possible. Do not assume that our descriptions of difficulty are overstatements. This park has dangerous terrain, and weather conditions are changeable and sometimes extreme. Off-trail hiking in Gros Morne may be more difficult than anything you have ever experienced—a cross between the terrain of the Rockies and the Arctic with low cloud, high winds, sodden ground, impassable brush, large animals, false trails, biting flies, and driving rain thrown in for fun.

For information about possible hazards in the park and how you can avoid them, talk to park personnel. Please be careful, enjoy your visit, and help us to protect the wildness of Gros Morne National Park.

High winds roil clouds over Bonne Bay, a weather change in the offing.

A YEAR IN GROS MORNE

SEASONS DIFFER SO MUCH FROM PLACE TO PLACE IN NORTH America that what constitutes a normal spring or autumn is consistent neither north to south, nor east to west, nor even from year to year. It has been said that the words *wind*, *water*, and *weather* share the same linguistic ancestry. If so, etymology and meteorology have definitely come to an understanding: Wind and water are by far the most important components of weather for anyone visiting the park.

Gros Morne's summers are never so hot and humid as to be unpleasant, and they are certainly not too long. Autumns are extended and sunny. Winters bring strong winds and deep snow. Springs race ahead and bump into the coming summer. Gros Morne National Park lies between 49° and 50° north latitude, about the same latitude as the cities of Vancouver, Winnipeg, Ulaanbaatar, Kiev, Prague, and Paris.

Events may differ by a week or two annually, but what follows is the usual course of a year at Gros Morne National Park.

UNSTABLE JANUARY

This is the beginning of real winter. The days are short, and frost slowly extends icy fingers into the ground. However, there is almost always a thaw near the end of January to melt winter back for a couple of days.

Snow mounds higher with each storm. After midmonth the land is usually deeply snowbound and Bonne Bay is frozen over. The sea remains open, but ice swathes the shoreline. Cold air and open ocean create unstable weather, and this can be an unpleasant time of year for driving, with occasional freezing rain and snow-covered black ice. Most ponds are frozen over, but some brooks and boggy areas are still too soft for off-trail cross-country skiing. Radio and television remind people that the greatest cause of drowning in this province of boaters is actually snowmobiles that break through the ice.

Most birds quit the park as winter approaches. Even gulls leave as the sea freezes over. Of the loyal species, the most prominent are those with the least camouflage: crows and ravens. Anyone who visits the park area will soon notice that outside every house is a box for garbage bags. There are several really good reasons for this: roaming dogs, very strong winds, and inquisitive birds. Any unsheltered garbage is quickly shredded. Crows spend most of the winter in gangs, hanging around town waiting for something edible to happen, yelling at each other, and scolding cats. Ravens are more reserved. They are usually seen singly or in pairs on the ice, on the mountains, or in open country looking like holes punched into the snowy back-

Fast-moving water often remains open all winter.

Backcountry ski routes lead to scenery inaccessible in summer.

ground. They fly noisy acrobatic duels through the quiet sky, or chuckle and gronk to their partners in graceful aerial dances, high above the cold white ground.

Cold darkens the needles of conifers to a sombre green-black and the landscape becomes a monochrome of angular branches and dark swaths of forest afloat in a sea of white. Hillside birch forests resemble a severe crew-cut, the pale crowns of hills shining through a twiggy stubble. In the bright of the day there are almost no shadows on the snowy ground, and hillocks, hollows, and even distances become hard to judge. With swirling snow the effect is almost hypnotic, a floating disconnection from the outside world as sights and sounds are muffled by white and one is forced into the company of one's inner thoughts—where, with any luck, things are a bit warmer.

FEBRUARY — THE COLDEST MONTH

For fans of frostbite, this is the best month to experience real ear-freezing, nose-burning, eye-watering, foot-numbing, lung-stinging cold. Although it may not get as bitter here as in some other parts of Canada, humidity often makes low temperatures bone chilling. The weather usually stabilizes in February, and the cross-country ski season begins in earnest.

Harbours freeze over early in the month, and the sea becomes a mass of white blocks as Gulf pack ice moves in. Storm winds exceeding 100 kilometres per hour drive snow off open ground and into the forest and valleys, and far higher winds rake the fjord canyons. Hard snowdrifts build up, and swirling ice crystals rattle off clothing and sting exposed skin. Trout River

Gulch can be a nightmare to drive through at this time of year. Even when there is no snow falling anywhere in the park, snow gusts off the top of the Tablelands and billows in blinding clouds at road level. Caribou feeding in herds in the lowlands around Sally's Cove and St. Pauls scratch down through crusty snow to reach the lichens. Entire herds appear and disappear like ghosts in the swirling flurries.

Ice pans cover the sea in winter.

Woodcutting is in full swing in park domestic harvest blocks and enclave community forests. Snowmobiles whine across ponds and lakes, their trails paralleling the roadside for kilometres. Drivers must be constantly on the lookout for snowmobiles—they can appear from nowhere and dart across the road like moose on a summer night.

Ice thickens on lakes, reaching 60 centimetres or more. Snow acts as an insulating blanket, but where it is blown away the soil freezes a metre or more deep. Plants cannot draw water from frozen soil, so buds and branches exposed to the strong cold winds dry and die—the "freezer burn" technique of pruning. For anyone travelling over brooks and lakes it is never safe to assume that ice is solid. Currents at rapids and warmer water upwelling from the depths of lakes can eat away at the bottom of the ice, leaving it dangerously thin.

The Tickle, off Norris Point, is the narrow entrance to the East Arm of Bonne Bay. It remains open through most of the winter as a steaming black hole in the ice. During the coldest weather it temporarily ices over, but tidal currents that flow in and out of the bay and the slightly warmer water that circulates from below soon open it up again. Because no ferry could operate in winter, people used to cross between Woody Point and Norris Point on foot or by dogsled. Snowmobiles and the occasional truck still do so—despite the risk.

Northern lights occur throughout the year, but seem most appropriate shimmering in the brittle cold of winter's darkness. At times the light fades until it resembles thin clouds. Then it swells into searchlights that scan the starry sky, or crumples into white curtains that all but rustle in the solar "wind." The entire fabric of the aurora seems to hang from the North Star and cloak the Big Dipper, the signposts of the Northern Hemisphere. Cold nights often throw a bright halo around the moon as fine clouds of ice crystals scatter and refract its silvery light. A full moon is usually so bright that it is easy to ski at night.

Pic à Tenerife and other difficult routes reward skiers with spectacular views.

© Michael Burzynski

MARCH — CROSS-COUNTRY SKIERS' MONTH

The third month usually starts out cold, but skies are clear and the skiing is great. When the Spring Equinox is reached on the 21st, day and night are of equal length, and day begins to pull into the lead. Recreational snowmobiling is in full roar, with hordes of machines fanning out across the snow. Snowmobile trails weave through the trees, stitching communities and the surrounding forest tightly together. People are out each day cutting next year's firewood and lumber, and most transport their logs on snowmobile-pulled sleighs. Trees are cut for domestic use in designated harvesting blocks within the park. As the month passes, more and more logs pile up along roadsides to be picked up by trucks. At Trout River and Rocky Harbour a few ponies are still used in the woods, reminders of an older and quieter time.

Snowshoe hares are snared in the enclaves and in the park's domestic cutting blocks, and people are often seen on foot or on snowmobile carrying several. These fresh *rabbits* (frozen solid with their ears, hair, snowshoes, and other appendages still firmly attached) are sometimes available in local stores.

Quieter pastimes such as snowshoeing, cross-country skiing, and skating are also popular at this time of year, and March is usually the best month to be out and experiencing the different types of snow. On the coldest days, dry powdery crystals crunch and squeak underfoot, refusing to compact into snowballs and flurrying across the ground with every wind. Loose snow blows away, leaving an icy crust across the landscape. In places, tracks show that the crust can bear even a moose's weight, but a short distance away the hoofprints punch through to the powdery snow beneath. Sometimes bright drops of blood speckle the snow where a moose or caribou has been scraped by breaking through the crust.

This is a good time of year for tracking. Pawprints can last for days, and the transient events of their making are recorded for anyone to read. For example, where a snowshoe hare has hopped down one snowbank then tried to bound up the next, only to lose its footing in deep snow and fall backward, imprints a moment of clumsiness on the white canvas of winter. Willow ptarmigan make plump ploughing tracks as they shuffle through powder snow between trees, and leave a zipper-like trail of meticulous pigeon-toed footprints in harder snow. Tracks and trails tell stories of browsing, of hunting, of escape, and of death.

The forest is hushed at this time of year, as though birds and even breezes are frozen into silence. Each breath is visible and invigorating—the air so cold that it feels thick. Exhalations heavy with water vapour solidify into icicles on beards and moustaches. Fine ice crystals sprout on eyebrows, eyelashes, and clothing, and eyelids stick together as tears freeze in the corners of wind-stung eyes. The air is sharp and pure; the landscape white and black and smooth. Pristine beauty rewards the ache of cold.

Water looms black beneath glass-clear ice. Sunlight is sliced by the edges of the cracks, shooting prisms of colour glinting and flashing against the black water below. Bubbly milk-white ice hangs from the lips of waterfalls. Yellow ice, stained by soil acids, builds ragged sheets beneath cliffside seeps. And at

Digging out a backcountry warden cabin.

Workhorses are still seen in some communities.

the mouths of springs, bulges of smooth ice glow with an inner untouchable sapphire blue.

Warmer days bring fluffy new snow. It drifts down lazily in clumps and sticks to branches and overhead wires in large cottony masses. At first decorative, it soon becomes serious, weighing down boughs, bending saplings to the ground, and obliterating all tracks and trails through the forest. Snowbanks sliced by ploughs and snowblowers reveal a frozen layered chronology of crusts left by brief thaws and the soft snow of intervening storms—all outlined in brown by accumulated road grit.

The rumble of waterfalls is heard beneath icy sheaths as rivers begin to melt their way through the blanket of winter. Black rushing holes open in the snow along brooks, and ice "wine glasses" dangle from twigs just above the water's surface. Tree buds plumpen, and birds become noisily active in the branches. White willow ptarmigan balance precariously in saplings, stretching for tender buds—sometimes overreaching and tumbling in a flail of wings to the snow below.

APRIL — FIRST STIRRINGS OF SPRING

Ten-Mile Pond is a long but easy ski.

© Michael Burzynski

Offshore the ice is usually still solid, or at most riven by a few blackwater leads. As the month progresses, wind breaks up the icepack, widening the leads and sometimes pushing the ice out of sight for days. Overnight it returns, crushing against the shore and filling the sea to the horizon. As the ice moves back and forth with the changing wind, large pressure ridges build up at Sally's Cove, Broom Point, and wherever else there are shallow reefs. Some piles of sea ice are more than 20 metres high, resembling icebergs. In bays the ice is usually still solid, and snowmobiles cross the harbours and coves. Occasionally a seal humps out of the water onto the edge of a lead to loll in the sun.

As the ice edge retreats northward, hundreds of thousands of harp seals migrate from the Gulf of St. Lawrence past the park coastline ready to bear their young on the ice. Early in the month sealing begins off Trout River and other places along the coast where it is possible to walk or boat out to the harp seal whelping pans. This hunt is for large seals, and both the meat and pelts are used.

Ravens start building big twiggy nests along the coastal cliffs. Crows are doing the same in the tops of trees. Bald eagles return as soon as there is open water, and ducks, gulls, and occasional flights of Canada geese follow in their wake. Eagles often perch at the ice edge in Bonne Bay eating fish that they have caught—hulking over the gulls and ravens that wait nearby for scraps. Starlings welcome the longer days with song, mimicking everything from native birds to cats and whistles. A few robins sometimes appear in the first week of April, but they are sometimes disappointed—or worse. As far as robins are concerned, it's the early bird that catches the frostbite. What is unimaginatively called "freezing rain" on the mainland becomes a *glitter storm* on the island. Although beautiful to see, these storms encrust trees with sheaves of ice, breaking limbs with the weight and making life miserable for hungry forest animals.

When spring finally reaches Gros Morne, it comes on the wings of returning birds. Flocks of American robins, northern flickers, fox sparrows, song sparrows, common snipe, goldeneyes, northern pintails, black ducks, ospreys, northern harriers, and others arrive in waves until early June.

The sight and sound of birds taking back the countryside from winter is accompanied by another seasonal milestone—the first spring flowers poking up between snowpatches. Sun-yellow coltsfoot usually heaves out of the thawed soil around foundations and ditches in the second week of April. In a few more weeks, roadside banks are golden with their blooms. Although not a native wildflower, the bright early flowers of coltsfoot are a welcome sight at the end of the long winter. Less visible is another early flower: the minute blooms of dwarf mistletoe show triplets of yellow anthers amid the tangled branches of the black spruce that they parasitize.

© Michael Burzynski

Bald eagles perch near a hole in the ice in Bonne Bay.

As the countryside melts out of its deep freeze, small streams and rivers become boiling torrents. Large boulders tumble down riverbeds, and great quantities of cobbles, gravel, sand, and silt are washed downstream. Ice blocks swirl in the current and crash against banks, bulldoze across bars, and knock bark and lower limbs off trees. Ice scars tree trunks a metre or more above summer water level. Alders and willow saplings are bent flat and stripped of their bark as icy water scours its way downstream during meltout. Rivers and brooks break up in earnest, with long strips of dark rushing water cutting courses through the otherwise snow-covered landscape.

In late winter and early spring, as the days get warmer, moist snow falls atop the existing blanket in large puffy flakes. When the wind is just right, tiny clumps of sticky snow are flipped over. Snow clings to snow, and the clumps are slightly higher than their surroundings. This makes an even larger surface for the wind to push on, and the lumps flip over again, and again, and again…. The snowy automatons tumble downwind across the countryside, getting bigger as they go. Usually they roll downhill, but if the wind is

© Michael Burzynski

Flood-swollen waterfall on the Lomond River.

strong enough they sometimes ascend slight inclines. As they roll they leave trails—dozens of widening tracks all leading in the same direction, each headed by a rolling clump of snow ranging from tennis ball to beach ball size. Then, as quickly as they were animated, the herd of snowballs stops dead— because the wind drops, or the balls have become too heavy to stay in motion.

The days are lengthening and warmer, so it is easy to take long off-trail ski trips—if one is wary of the melting ice. Some days are even T-shirt weather, but beware of sunburn (especially from sunlight reflected onto normally burn-proof areas such as ear lobes and the underside of your chin). Ice is more persistent in the bays. A Coast Guard icebreaker usually works its way up the Gulf and comes into Bonne Bay, breaking channels through the melting ice. The bay is often ice free within a week. Unfortunately, ice pans are created

Snow rollers on the Visitor Centre lawn.

by this, pans that would not occur during the slower natural melting of the bay. They blow against the shore, damage wharves, and sometimes drastically reduce shoreline organisms. Ice breakup galvanizes everyone; summer is coming, fishing gear is readied, boats are put in the water, and businesses prime for the coming visitor season.

Deep holes melt out around the boles of trees as bark absorbs then reflects solar heat. Meltwater trickles into cracked asphalt, freezes and expands, heaving the roads into bumps and potholes. Thaws sap snowbanks, melting gritty holes and sending tinkling cascades of ice sliding down their flanks. Lakes are still frozen, but meltwater puddles on the thinning ice, and inky open water gapes near the shores. On the lowlands the snow gets slushy and patches of soil are showing through. However, winter is not finished with the park yet, and there is often a slushy snowfall in April, May, or even June. Caribou move back to the highlands in preparation for calving.

Late April and early May bring the start of the lobster fishing season. The season is often delayed for a few weeks by drifting sea ice that can endanger boats, crews, and gear, and the radio is usually alive with reports about the ice edge. Lobsters boiling in the pot are a sure sign of spring, as is the mandatory removal of studded snow tires by the end of the month.

MAY — THE CAMPERS RETURN

Black bears leave their dens at the beginning of the month, and clumsy cubs are introduced to the outside world. Flocks of robins hop across open

Small flats are the usual boats in the inshore fishery.

ground in search of insects and worms, and the eerie vibrato "calls" of snipe float through the evening air to announce that spring is officially in progress.

Telemark and downhill skiers find enough snow on the flanks of the Tablelands for a few runs. Unfortunately, this area can be extremely dangerous. Boulders are exposed by melting snow, avalanches occur when large cornices overhanging the cirques become unstable, and melting snow bridges conceal deep rocky gorges filled with rushing water. Although the lowlands are thawing quickly, the highlands are usually still snow-covered and frozen.

Ice candles grow overnight in sodden ground, tearing the soil and heaving plants right out of the earth. Each cold night adds a new layer to the ice candles, and the expanded soil is brittle and insubstantial underfoot. Offshore, rotten ice crumbles from the edges of grounded pans, slushing into the sea and turning it milky as fresh meltwater and salty seawater mingle. The last snowbanks fall apart with a tinkling and sparkling of ice gems forged by sunlight. Water is regaining its mobility, and everywhere there are drips and puddles and rushing freshets. Piles of soggy snow slip from tree branches where they have roosted throughout the winter. Green shoots spike up through the matted brown vegetation of melt patches, immune to nightly frosts and the threat of further snow.

Purple saxifrage.

Mayflower, or trailing arbutus.

Moss campion.

By the second week, arctic-alpine plants are flowering in the Tablelands and on coastal cliffs. Lapland rosebay, a wild dwarf rhododendron, bears masses of magenta flowers that seem far too large for so small a bush. Tight clumps of rosebay grow scattered across the lower flanks of the Tablelands, and in places form low pink hedges. Purple saxifrage has smaller magenta flowers, but they are every bit as bright, and dot the landscape with the promise of summer. Large creamy-white blossoms cover carpets of dark, leathery, arrow-shaped leaves where mountain avens bloom. These last two species grow on cliffs and in lime-rich soils along the coast and in the Tablelands area. North of the park, in the limestone barrens near Bellburns and Port au Choix, they create scenes that resemble an Arctic island. The season is slightly retarded farther north on the Great Northern Peninsula—stretching spring flowering out an extra couple of weeks. Sweet gale, alder, and trailing arbutus are soon

Mountain avens.

Speckled alder catkins.

Marsh marigold.

Laurentian, or bird's-eye primrose.

in flower, and by the third week marsh marigold brightens wetlands throughout the park with its massed yellow cups.

The Victoria Day Weekend, around the third week in May, heralds the start of the new visitor season. A few hardy campers arrive with tents, trailers, and recreational vehicles for the first park visit of the year.

Spindly mayflies and nondescript brown moths take to the air as the melt continues. Crocuses show their heads in gardens, spiders and snails move about on patches of bare ground, and the first midges swarm in the cool air. Beetles wander around the base of trees and under rocks looking cold and more than a bit stiff from their long frozen winter. Mite webs and fungus filaments knit mats of dead leaves and branches together beneath the melting snow. In meadows, the thaw exposes networks of tightly packed grass—the tunnels where meadow voles have lived and fed throughout the winter.

Chickadees become more talkative, and other birds call to the awakening forest. Hills flush with a faint pink as birches prepare to open their leaves. Icy mists hover above black water as streams melt their winter crust. Hoarfrost clings softly to the branches of surrounding trees. In the reviving forest, snow-bowed spruce boughs bounce back. Snapped branches ooze resin and sap, and the dark conifers green up as their needles rehydrate.

By the end of the month, spring is in full bloom with Laurentian primrose, moss campion, wild strawberry, rhodora, and many other plants. Cow moose prepare to give birth, and drive off last year's young. Although almost fully grown, the yearlings appear forlorn and confused, and often loiter along roadsides or wander into towns. As many as 60 moose, mostly yearlings, have been counted in one morning drive between Wiltondale and Rocky Harbour at this time of year.

JUNE — LONG DAYS & NORTHERN WILDFLOWERS

Toads start calling from ponds that they have colonized. Spring in Newfoundland is silent compared to the deafening amphibian chorus of the mainland, but these isolated toads do their best to trill in the spring. Most caribou bear their calves in the first weeks of the month, usually near the highland snowbeds, but occasionally on boggy lowlands and in the forest. Ptarmigan and Arctic hares are also raising their young, and are most vulnerable to disturbance at this time of year.

Atop Gros Morne and other highlands, diapensia, an arctic cushion plant, raises cup-shaped flowers above its densely overlapping leaves, and heavy bumblebees flounder through the cool air. The first weeks of June also see the awakening of hibernating butterflies. Dark mourning cloaks float through the sky like the dry leaves that their underwings mimic, Yellow-and-black-striped tiger swallowtails look decidedly tropical as they flit over brown meadows whose plants are still trying to shake winter's torpor. Milbert's tortoiseshells, green commas, and red admirals add a touch of red to the air, recalling the colours of autumn when they last flew. Timed to the awakening of insects is the return of the warblers, brightening this northern forest with their southern colours and songs

There is still a lot of snow on the highlands. The last roadside snowpatch lingers at the top of the Southeast Hills, often surviving until mid-month.

As the days warm and the snow melts in the woods, brown water swells even small brooks into raging torrents. Alder, poplar, and willow buds burst

© Anne Marceau, GMNP

Cow moose in spring.

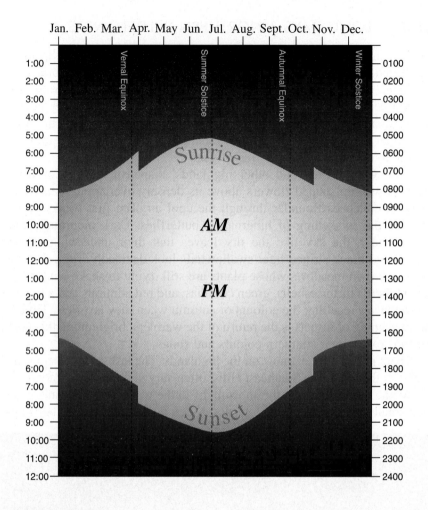

Jan. Feb. Mar. Apr. May Jun. Jul. Aug. Sept. Oct. Nov. Dec.

Vernal Equinox
Summer Solstice
Autumnal Equinox
Winter Solstice

Sunrise

AM

Sunset

1:00	0100
2:00	0200
3:00	0300
4:00	0400
5:00	0500
6:00	0600
7:00	0700
8:00	0800
9:00	0900
10:00	1000
11:00	1100
12:00	1200
1:00	1300
2:00	1400
3:00	1500
4:00	1600
5:00	1700
6:00	1800
7:00	1900
8:00	2000
9:00	2100
10:00	2200
11:00	2300
12:00	2400

PM

Daylength changes throughout the year. The jog in this graph indicates the onset of Daylight-Saving Time.

Showy lady's-slipper.

© Michael Burzynski

Yellow lady's-slipper.

© Michael Burzynski

open, releasing catkins that droop flacidly as they strew clouds of pollen to the wind. Sometimes in the first weeks of June, spruce pollen dusts every outside surface and forms yellow windrows on lakes and bays. Each tiny ornamented pollen grain stuck to a car or washed up on a beach is a failed attempt at reproduction. Their vast numbers show how inefficient wind pollination is. Nevertheless, millions of pollen grains do find their mark, and in trees all around the park fertilized ovules quietly develop into seeds. Schools of capelin usually spawn on beaches in middle or late June and this is the best time to see the whales that follow them. Moose give birth to wobbly legged cinnamon-coloured calves throughout the month.

Hooded ladies'-tresses.

June 21st marks the Summer Solstice, the longest day of the year. Daylight lasts 16 hours and 13 minutes. From now until December 21st the days grow shorter. June is the begining of the visitor season in the park area. By the third week,

Calopogon, or marsh pink orchid.

Purple-fringed orchis.

Arethusa, or dragon's-mouth orchid

Northern bog-orchis.

Leafy white orchis.

summer staff are all at their stations, and park facilities and tourist operations are open.

JULY — ORCHID MONTH

Gros Morne Trail and the highland traverses are usually opened to hikers at the beginning of July. The first three weeks are the best time to see wildflowers — especially orchids such as pink lady's-slipper, yellow lady's-slipper, showy lady's-slipper, leafy white-orchis, purple-fringed orchis, dragon's-mouth orchid, bog pink, rose pogonia, and white bog-orchis.

Caribou crowd a Big Level snowbed in July.

Summer interpretive events such as guided walks on trails, evening programs at the theatre, campfires, and special events are available in different parts of the park, with some programs running every day of the week. These events are the best way to find out about the park's geology, its plants and animals, and its human history.

Summer is in full swing, and since it only lasts until September it is important to take full advantage of the long days. Hikers linger on trails and beaches well into the evening, strolling through hour-long sunsets. Strong winds are less frequent at this time of year.

Plants put on a spurt of growth that can almost be watched, and in the burgeoning greenery birds sing their territorial calls each dawn and dusk. Flowers are everywhere in the forest, on the barrens, and in the ditches, and accompanying them is an army of insect pollinators, herbivores, and predators. It is still possible to find fresh perfect leaves on trees, but caterpillars, fungi, bacteria, and wind will soon mark them.

Blue skies give way to a vast panorama of stars at night, and northern lights are not uncommon rippling across the black sky. There are even lights in the water. Tiny bioluminescent plants and animals spangle the bays and coves whenever a wave rolls in, or a boat or whale passes by. Just flipping over seaweed at the water's edge is usually enough to make them sparkle.

By midmonth, lobster pots are out of the water and piled ashore, and the season is over. The water is

Red crowberry.

Partridgeberry or mountain cranberry.

Bakeapple or cloudberry.

Dwarf Arctic bramble or *plumboys*.

© Michael Burzynski

Black crowberry or *blackberry*.

© Michael Burzynski

Blueberry.

© Michael Burzynski

bioluminescent plants and animals spangle the bays and coves whenever a wave rolls in, or a boat or whale passes by. Just flipping over seaweed at the water's edge is usually enough to make them sparkle.

By midmonth, lobster pots are out of the water and piled ashore, and the season is over. The water is warming up, and paddlers and swimmers start to use the sandy beaches. Backcountry hikers at this comfortable time of year sometimes forget how different the weather on the highlands can be, and are surprised at how fast it changes from warm and clear to dangerously cold, wet, and misty.

On those highlands the caribou are taking maximum advantage of the late-melting snowpatches to escape the heat and the flies. Early in the month, rock ptarmigan roam the hills with their new chicks, and Arctic hares with their leverets. On the lowlands, moose wade out into ponds to feed on sweet yellow pondlily rhizomes. Minke whales continue to cruise along shore, and harbour seals bask on exposed rocks at low tide. The southward migration of shorebirds from Arctic and Subarctic nesting grounds begins in the third week of July and lasts into early October. These birds show up in small flocks along the shore, especially at St. Pauls marsh. The earliest migrants are usually whimbrels; later come various sandpipers and plovers. Adult birds move south first, and are later followed by their young.

July is usually ushered out by a hail of large mayflies that hatch

and the sides of buildings. Where they rest they leave behind carbon copies of themselves in the form of dried false-imago skins. Alone among insects, mayflies have both a subadult and an adult flying stage. Each drab hollow skin marks where a mayfly flew ashore and reached full maturity. Abandoning their brief "adolescence," they shed even the lining of their breathing spiracles, which trail like white threads from the cracked skins out of which the adult mayflies emerge. Adult mayflies are harmless, and do not even have functional mouthparts. They live only a few days, just long enough to mate and lay eggs. Then they are finished, like the month itself.

AUGUST —
THE WARMEST WEATHER

The warmest weather of the year occurs during August, and the water in brooks, streams, and bays becomes downright pleasant for swimming. Along this coast, a fortnight without rain would be a drought—but lawns rarely go brown. Biting flies are not often a problem along the coast or in the open because constant breezes keep them away. But during calm weather, or in the sheltered forest of valleys, blackflies and mosquitoes can be a great annoyance. If the flies are going to be bad, this is the month they usually choose to do it.

Strawberries and several species of blueberries are ripe, and roadsides near bogs are lined with

© Michael Burzynski

Stream water is tinted by soil acids.

the cars of bakeapple pickers. People wander bogs all along the Great Northern Peninsula with sticky fingers and bags of soft yellow berries. Park campgrounds are alive with visitors, but rarely is there difficulty in finding a site, even at this peak season. A lot of people are using the trails, so most of the large mammals move into the forest to avoid disturbance. However, early risers still have a good chance of seeing wildlife on trails and along roadsides.

Early month sees the southward shorebird migration in full swing, with hundreds of birds feeding and roosting in St. Pauls marsh and in the muddy shallows around Lomond and Glenburnie. Bald eagle chicks are fledged, and leave their aerie to learn hunting with their parents. Ospreys continue their hovering fishing expeditions in shallows.

Late summer is the best time to look at tidepools along the shore. The water is warm and seaweed growth is lush. Among the green, red, brown, and golden fronds are tiny hermit crabs and pink-frilled sea slugs, as well as the usual anemones, winkles, whelks, shrimp and small fish. People sun on the sand at Western Brook, or walk for kilometres beside the dunes at Shallow Bay, where children play in the water and snorkellers watch sea life in the swaying eelgrass.

Salmon are in the rivers, lying in pools sculling slowly with their wide tails, awaiting a rainfall that will let them ascend further upstream, closer to their spawning grounds. If the water gets too warm it can kill the fish. On the highlands, caribou are also trying to deal with the heat. Most snowbeds have withered away, and caribou seek out the highest points of land to catch a breeze that will help cool them and keep away flies. Sometimes they stand one per rock knob like statues on pedestals. At other times they crowd twenty deep on a small hillock, branching antlers resembling dead tuckamore from a distance. They only move to shake off the flies, and their snorts and sneezes can be heard from some distance.

There are a thousand small things in the forest to be savoured

© Michael Burzynski

Mushroom "fairy rings" at the Visitor Centre.

Canoeing on Bakers Brook Pond.

slowly at this time: backlit leaves aglow in a shaft of sunlight, a shred of birchbark fluttering against a velvety smooth trunk, the smell of a woodland brook, the cool green of a moss cushion, and pearl-like rows of dew on a morning spider web.

Boats are on the water with gulls wheeling and crying in their wakes, kayaks bob in the bays, kaleidoscopic kites flutter and dive in the breeze, and bright clothing weaves through the forest accompanied by drifting snatches of chatter and laughter. Breezes waft scents of grass, of seaweed, warm balsam fir, crushed wild mint, mushrooms, and forest soil. The air vibrates with the buzz of bees, the whine of flies, and the rustle of hunting dragonflies. Soil is soft underfoot, and warm zephyrs stroke the hairs on your arm—this is summer, a good time to be alone with your senses.

By the end of the month herring and mackerel school into the bays, and with them come white-sided dolphins, whales, occasional sharks, and seiners.

SEPTEMBER — HIKING INTO AUTUMN

Raspberries are ripe, and loose on the bush. Bears sweep in armfuls of canes and graze the berries from the top, leaving a trail of flattened stems. Canada geese fly through the park on their way south, their honks preceding them. Often flocks stop to feed on the newly greened hillsides of late snowpatches on the Long Range and in ponds on the coastal lowlands.

By Labour Day the park's summer season is winding down, and some facilities close or reduce services. Gardeners start to worry about early frosts. Certainly there will be frost in hollows and cold nights on the highlands, and there can even be a dusting of snow on the mountains as early as the second week of the month.

Bull moose during the rut.

Shorter daylength tricks a few flowers into blooming again. Wild strawberry, bunchberry (*crackerberry*), twinflower, violets, purple lousewort, diapensia, moss campion, and others often produce a small number of flowers in the fall instead of waiting for spring.

With cool nights come fall colours in the forest. But the first leaves to change are on the highlands. About mid-month the small birches and willows turn golden, and low-growing blueberries and Arctic bearberry become a scarlet carpet. This flush of colour can even be seen from the lowlands. It is a good time to climb Gros Morne, since the uphill slog is cooler, most of the flies are gone, the heaths are colourful, and caribou have returned to the mountain with the decline of visitors. The Long Range Traverse is also more comfortable because the days are warm and clear, and the nights are crisp.

In cool years, the snow on the Tablelands will now have shrunk to a spot, and only a few small patches of last year's snow remain on the Long Range. On the 21st of the month comes the Autumn Equinox. Now nights begin to get longer than days, and winter is nigh. There is still a chance of a week or two of warm clear Indian Summer, often following a cool wet spell.

Waterthrushes, warblers, sparrows, and other small birds flock in preparation for their southward migration. They pass through the trees in waves, feeding and moving short distances during the day, then flying fast and unseen by night, their peeps and chirps coming out of the dark sky like sounds from the stars. American pipits and horned larks are everywhere on

Caribou feeding on the lowlands in autumn.

the highlands, and small flocks of rock and willow ptarmigan take advantage of the last warm days to gorge on buds and berries.

Cream-coloured hemlock looper moths flutter from spruce and fir boughs with every breeze. Tangled mountain cranberry (called *partridgeberry* in much of Newfoundland) mats are laden with tart scarlet berries—still too green on the underside to eat.

Fairy rings sprout from lawns around the middle of the month, each circle of mushrooms outlining where the actual fungus lives beneath the soil. They will last for about three weeks. Squirrels, slugs, and caribou eat large numbers of mushrooms—even those toxic to humans—and squirrels even gather and store them in branches to dry for later consumption.

By the third week of September only a few species of flowers are still out: shrubby cinquefoil, papery white pearly everlasting, blue and magenta asters, goldenrod, white Canada burnet, and Canada thistles. Along roadsides coarse coltsfoot leaves flash silver undersides in the wind, and cow parsnip umbels stand high above the shrivelling roadside plants atop thick bamboo-like stems.

Most insects are either dying off or are in hibernation. Hairy black flies snuggle into the cracks around windows and doors, crowding attics and outbuildings. Jays, warblers, and other birds scrabble at the walls of buildings, trying to nab flies, spiders, and moths as they search for crevices. Dragonflies survive to the end of the month, flying lower and more slowly as they starve. Early mornings see them covered in cold dew. They cling

Autumn colours at Southeast Brook Falls.

tightly to the wilting vegetation with wings aquiver in an attempt to warm flight muscles for one last search for food. Only the nymphs will survive to next year, safe on the bottom of streams and ponds. Butterflies are almost finished. Only a few leaf-brown mourning cloaks flutter around on warm days, searching for a secure place to spend the winter. Dime-sized yellow orb spiders hang heavily from their webs, their larders almost bare and the cold seeping into their bodies. The adults will soon perish, but their young will survive the long winter.

Gales herald the end of summer, as autumn blows in on the wind. The trees have a definite tattered look. Each leaf has been riddled by feeding insects, is contorted with galls, or patched with mould. Their job done and their lifespan run, hardwood trees shut down their leaves with a flourish of colour, then drop them. Soon the red and yellow leaves of fall glow dimly through a lacy icing of hoarfrost. The leaves brown and shrivel, and are tugged from the trees by wind to be scattered far from home. The air is cold and clear, and frost nips harder each evening. Potatoes are dug from roadside gardens.

Fluorescent orange dollops of witches' butter seem to ooze out of dead softwood trunks. As leaves wither, this small, gelatinous, wood-rotting fungus is one of the few splashes of colour left in the forest. By month's end, occasional light snowfalls turn mountaintops white, but the snow usually melts by the end of the day.

OCTOBER — FROST AND ANTLERS

Fall colours continue into early October. Daylength also causes changes in the colour of ptarmigan, and by the third week of October these birds are already mostly white. Occasional snows frost dark hilltops and filter down into the yellow birches on their flanks. Then comes a wind, and by next day the colourful leaves are all gone.

Moose return to trails that they abandoned as summer visitors increased, and are seen in large numbers on the highlands. Moose are preparing for rut, and bulls can be cantankerous. Bulls have rubbed all of the velvet off their antlers by late September, and their tines look almost yellow. Throughout the forest and wetlands moose scrape shallow muddy pits about a metre in diameter. They urinate in these, then rub to spread the "perfume." Although irresistible to other moose, the pong from these wallows is strong enough to make one's eyes water. The wallows become crossroads in the moose highway system. Spring's calves are almost full size by this time of year, and will remain with their mothers throughout the winter.

Caribou started to move down onto the lowlands in the first half of September. The rut with its mating activity is in full swing by October, and will last until December. Stag caribou on the lowlands joust with each other and mate with females as the rut proceeds. Hundreds of caribou feed in herds on the wetlands from Green Point north. Young stags often engage in shoving exercises, and the clatter of antlers rings across the lowlands. Larger stags usually only have to turn their heads in a threatening way to scare away smaller opponents. When big stags clash, it usually only lasts a few seconds. The furious pushing and shaking ends with the loser disengaging and trotting away, conceding defeat to the stag with the better traction.

Gangs of crows are forming again, carousing across the sky in squabbling raucous mobs. They

Blueberry leaves blaze red in autumn near Bakers Brook.

© Michael Burzynski

Brooding sky over Gros Morne.

Mike Potter, GMNP

Sun breaking through storm clouds, Gros Morne.

© Michael Burzynski

strut around town, pulling apart garbage bags and cawing unkind things at cats and dogs. Ravens fly in pairs, engaging in tight aerial acrobatics where the wind is strongest.

Orange mountain ash berries (*dogberries*) dangle from branches everywhere. Bunchberries brighten the forest floor, soon to be pulled apart as birds and voles feast on them. Bears are busy taking advantage of all the fruit. They pull down small trees for their berries, and leave large droppings that look as though someone has tipped a berry bucket. Glossy-black and flabby with fat, bears also spend a lot of time on the barrens eating blueberries and cranberries. In this way large numbers of seeds are moved from place to place, a sort of transit service with the fare being the sweet flesh of the berries.

Beautiful despite their name, bright yellow slime-moulds creep together to form tiny spore-bearing "mushrooms" on the leaf-strewn forest floor. The intricate architectural shapes of these minute fruiting bodies can only be appreciated with a hand lens. Clumps of shaggy mane mushrooms burst out of the soil, resembling huddles of tiny bedraggled parasols. They are common along roadsides and in lawns where bulldozers have buried logs. Within a few days of their appearance, the mushroom caps darken and then deliquesce—dissolving into sticky smelly black soup. This unpleasant mess is a spa for flies, which frolic and wade in the mushroom puddles. Shaggy mane spores cling to the flies, and are eventually spread far away from the original mushrooms.

Trees are bare by mid-month, and the bulk of the migratory birds have passed through. Most ferns, grasses, and herbaceous plants die back, withdrawing life into roots, rhizomes, bulbs, and tubers buried safely underground. Late in the month bears too head underground, seeking out small caves, upturned tree roots, or dense birch clumps to dig into. There they bed down for their winter sleep. In years when berry crops are thin, bears den earlier. Although they will move if disturbed during the winter, usually they stay in the same place until spring.

The first heavy frosts on the lowlands often occur in the second week of October. Frosts are a visual fanfare of crystal-fringed branches, tinkling puddle ice, and mist hovering low over ponds and streams. But some colour remains. The last of the trees to lose leaves are the larches. Their needles blaze orange-yellow for almost two weeks, then fall in a golden filigree around the base of each tree.

Lenticular cloud over Curzon Village.

© Michael Burzynski

NOVEMBER — WINTER'S ENTRY

October and November skies are spectacular, lighting up the escarpment of the Long Range. With alpenglow on the hills and caribou in the foreground amid yellow sedge clumps, an evening drive up Highway 430 can be spectacular.

The first storms of winter hurl huge piles of seaweed onto the beaches. This *killup* and *red moss* is gathered in October and November as a fertilizing mulch for vegetable gardens. Fast-melting snowfalls occur several times during the month. There is a smell of woodsmoke on the air, and talk of studded tires, four-wheel drives, and moose hunting. "Dijegitchyrmoosbye?" is a frequently heard conversational gambit—and by now most hunters have. Snowmobiles and sleighs are repaired, boats are hauled out of the water, and after midmonth the first lasting snow of winter may be on the ground.

Ice-caked trees along the shore of Western Brook Pond.

Caribou congregate near the highway south of St. Pauls, grazing their way through the tastiest pieces of seaweed on roadside gardens and nibbling at any cabbages, potatoes, or greens left in the ground. Most of the whales are gone from park area, but the occasional minke is seen offshore, and radio reports usually indicate that humpback whales are feeding on Arctic cod (*icefish*) in White Bay as the water chills. Within weeks they too will have to move south.

Caribou stags start to shed their antlers around midmonth. Females and young males will keep theirs until spring. The lowlands have turned from green to orange to brown. Although snow storms can come at any time during the month, lasting snow usually does not fall until after midmonth, sometimes as late as mid-December.

DECEMBER — THE DARKEST MONTH

The shortest day of the year is the 21st of December. This is the Winter Solstice, and the sun will shine for only 8 hours and 13 minutes. Although this is the darkest part of the year, things will soon brighten: from now until the Summer Solstice the days gradually get longer.

There is usually no dependable snow for skiing on the lowlands, but there is lots on the hills. Ponds and brooks are skimmed over with ice, but certainly not enough to hold weight. Even bogs remain unfrozen and are too mucky to cross. There is about an 80% chance of a white Christmas in the park area.

The last berries on the mountain ash trees are greedily picked off by European starlings and cedar waxwings. The period from December to April is a quiet time for birds. Few remain in the park as winter progresses, and they are more often heard than seen. A woodpecker's knock travels far

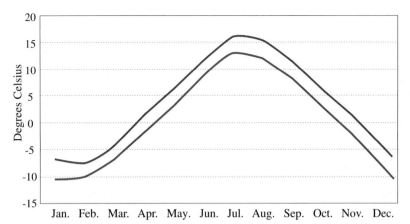

The highlands are cooler than the lowlands all year. The red line records the mean temperature at sea level, and the purple corresponds to the highlands (750 m elevation).

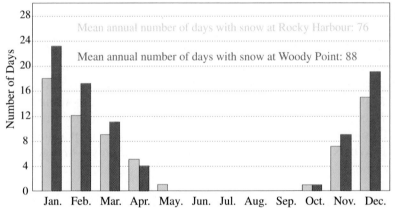

Mean annual number of days with snow at Rocky Harbour: 76

Mean annual number of days with snow at Woody Point: 88

Woody Point consistently receives more snowfall than the Rocky Harbour area.

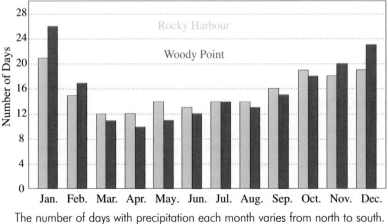

Rocky Harbour

Woody Point

The number of days with precipitation each month varies from north to south. Bonne Bay is a climatic dividing line. Graphs adapted from *Climate* by C. Banfield in *R. D. A. Gros Morne National Park*.

in the cold air, as do the whistles of crossbills as they fly over the icy forest. There has been an annual Christmas Bird Count in park area since 1971. The Bonne Bay count usually records between 20 and 40 species, and up to 3,400 individual birds. Of those, the gulls (herring, Iceland, and great black-backed), crows, common ravens, common redpolls, pine grosbeaks, white-winged crossbills, boreal and black-capped chickadees, and the introduced house sparrows and European starlings are the most dependable species.

THE LONG RANGE FORECAST

Temperatures: Warmest recorded in the park: 30°C; coldest: -36°C. February and March are the coldest months, July and August are the warmest. The highlands are usually about 4°C cooler than the lowlands, sometimes as much as 10°C cooler.

Frost-free Period: Maximum for the park is 150 days, 133 at Woody Point, 103 for Rocky Harbour.

Wind Speed: Prevailing winds blow from the southwest, but the worst storms are out of the east. The maximum recorded wind velocity was 150 kilometres per hour, but during one storm an anemometer at Western Brook Pond rated for winds of 200 kilometres per hour stopped recording and blew away. Needless to say, no one knows what the real wind record is for the park. Throughout the year, winds of 80 to 100 kilometres per hour are not unusual. Winds on the highlands are usually 2 to 2.5 times stronger than on the lowlands.

Precipitation: Some precipitation is usually recorded 200 days out of each year. Average annual precipitation at sea level is about 1,200 millimetres; on the highlands it is 2,750. Of that precipitation, the lowlands receives 400 to 450 centimetres of snow per year, and the highlands 800 to 1,000 centimetres (snowfall is measured in centimetres: 1 centimetre of snow is equivalent to 1 millimetre of rain). Low cloud becomes dense fog for hikers on the highlands. Low winter clouds often obscure the highlands for days.

THE WIND PREVAILS

At exposed headlands along the coast, wind blowing off the sea sometimes throws rocks uphill. In spring, before the grass and other plants sprout, anyone walking along these headlands will find flakes of shale hurled as much as 65 metres inland. At Salmon Point, near Rocky Harbour, it is not uncommon to find shoe-sized sandstone slabs weighing a couple of kilograms as far as 30 metres inland from the cliff edge!

Summer's gentler winds are usually welcome. They cool hikers and drive away flies. On beaches, breezes animate knee-high flurries of sand that rush around tickling the legs of walkers. Breezes also stir up rogue sand that seeks out pockets, camera equipment, and eyes. Stronger winds flip the tops off waves and blow foam against the shore in deep drifts. Frothy clumps of brown bubbles tumble or waft inland and cling to the tuckamore like wet snow. This foam, rich in marine organic matter, sometimes lasts for days. The day following a storm is usually clear and calm, but the sea remains agitated and roiling, hurling breakers against headlands and wharves.

Autumn colours the lowland barrens near Bakers Brook Pond, and moose, caribou, and bears feed there as winter approaches.

Common juniper stunted by living conditions in the Tablelands.

SCENIC ROOTS

HE SPECTACULAR SCENERY AND COMPLEX GEOLOGY OF the west coast of Newfoundland have led to a diversity of ecosystems and plant life unrivaled in the province. They also led to Gros Morne's prestigious UNESCO World Heritage Site designation. Many of the park's rock exposures, geological suites, and fossil assemblages are of international significance, attracting geologists, teachers and students, and interested amateurs from around the world.

The evolution of the park's scenery can be grouped into four main stages: the long story of bedrock formation, erosion that created a vast flat land surface, relatively recent glacial carving of the bedrock, and current geological processes. These are all easily explored in Gros Morne because of the sparse vegetation in many areas of the park.

THE OLDEST ROCK

We begin our tour of the distant past at Western Brook Pond, on a boat tour looking up at the cliffs of the Long Range Mountains. These massive cliffs are composed of the oldest rock in the park, a 1.25 billion year old fragment of the Canadian Precambrian Shield. It is a mix of igneous and metamorphic rocks—a plutonic complex. The metamorphic rocks are of both igneous (granite and gabbro) and sedimentary origin.

The oldest rock in the park forms the highlands of the Long Range.

NOTEPAD

The unifying Theory of Plate Tectonics describes how, over geological time, the crust of the earth has been mobile. The crust is cracked into a gigantic jigsaw with about 20 large and small rigid plates that float and shift on the plastic mantle. They form our continents and ocean basins. As these plates move, they grind past each other, collide, crumple together, and slide one below the other. Their jostles and shifts cause earthquakes and volcanoes, and also raise mountain chains. Plates melt when their edges plunge down into the mantle at subduction zones; they become larger where new rock is added to their edges at midocean spreading centres. At times, drifting plates coalesce and form supercontinents; when a supercontinent breaks apart, new oceans are created between new continents. The surface of the earth has changed continually since the crust formed 4.6 billion years ago, and still moves beneath us today.

Deformed and heated during the movements of crust and mantle over the eons, much of the granite has been altered into gneiss—a banded metamorphic rock. The rock that we see today lay deep within a massive range called the Grenville Mountains. By 650 million years ago these rocks were part of a supercontinent that contained most of the world's existing landmasses.

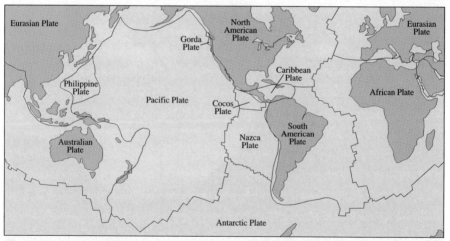

Through time, the earth's crust is constantly rearranged as huge plates of rock slowly move together or pull apart.

Hot convection currents in the mantle pulled at the overlying super-continent, stretching and cracking it. By about 600 million years ago the supercontinent containing the Long Range gneiss sundered along a sunken rift valley much like the East African Rift of today. Squeezed up from below, magma (molten rock) injected itself into cracks in the over-lying crust. There it cooled and hard-ened, sealing the cracks with diabase dykes. These deep rocks surfaced after 300 to 400 million years of ero-sion wore away the overlying moun-tains. Each dyke looks like a huge stripe up the 600- to 700-metre cliff faces, but this is only the thin edge of a sheet of rock that may run through the gneiss for kilometres. The diabase weathers more rapidly than the surrounding gneiss, producing steep ravines and waterfalls in the cliffs.

Southeast Hills roadcut.

© Michael Burzynski

Magma poured up through the diabase dykes, hardening at the surface as basalt, and an ocean filled the widening rift depression. Geologists call this proto-Atlantic ocean *Iapetus*. At this time western Newfoundland lay in the southern tropics.

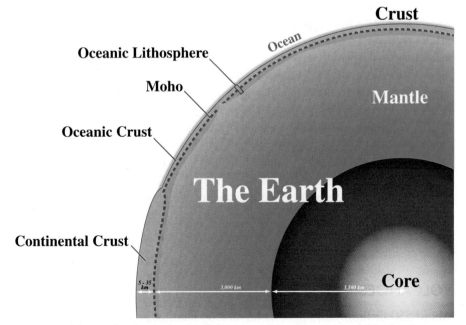

Anatomy of the earth. The thickness of the crust is greatly exaggerated in this diagram.

Green Gardens headlands are composed of pillow lavas, lava flows, and ash layers.

ANCIENT SEAFLOOR

The Southeast Hills roadcut is an ancient seabed—the floor of an ocean that opened and closed long before the Atlantic was born. This roadcut slices through a tilted section of the earliest sediments laid down in shallows along the margin of the Iapetus Ocean. On the right is 1,200 million year old (Precambrian) granite. For hundreds of millions of years erosion stripped away the granite, leaving a thin fossil soil made up of pink pebbles. Directly on top is ten metres of black gritty sandstone, probably also laid down on land. The sandstone grades into a nodular grey-brown limestone with marine fossils. This limestone represents the first sediment that accumulated on the edge of the growing Iapetus Ocean as it flooded the land here about 540 million years ago (Cambrian). This unconformity between Cambrian and Precambrian rocks represents a gap in the rock record of more than 500 million years.

VOLCANOES IN THE SEA

About 550 million years ago, as Iapetus opened, huge cauldrons of magma seethed beneath the newly forming oceanic crust, and lava poured out through cracks onto the sea bed. Seamounts, and perhaps volcanic islands, grew from the spewing lavas.

At Green Gardens, the old lava has weathered into a crumbly soil that supports lush grassy meadows (the rock is rich in calcium, potassium, sodium, and aluminium). The cliffs here are walls of grey-green and brown basalt with layers of volcanic sediment. Sea stacks rise from the water—portions of volcanic breccia headlands. This breccia formed when lava shattered as it quickly cooled and hardened underwater. White calcite later cemented the dark rock shards together, producing striking patterns of angular breccia. A nearby cliff is made up of reddish-brown trachyte. Thick green-grey layers in the headland by the staircase are *tuff*, a rock composed of layers of ash and stony debris that rained down during volcanic eruptions.

During the next 100 million years the ancient continent *Laurentia* (the core of North America) drifted northward. Sediments washed from the land and accumulated as a continental shelf. Some layers of sand, washed almost clean of minerals other than pure quartz, later solidified into quartzite. Sediment supply from the land eventually waned, and limy layers of shells and calcified algae began to accumulate, and now form limestone layers.

The face of Gros Morne mountain is marked with tilted rock ledges that show this pattern of accumulation. A hike up the mountain is a trip onto the ancient continental shelf. The mountain sits on Long Range gneiss (as seen in the cliffs of Ten Mile Pond), but the mountain itself is quartzite that was once sand beaches and bars along the western shore of Iapetus Ocean. Farther up the mountainside are narrow bands of shaly limestone that formed in deeper water, indicating that the sea was flooding the edge of the continent. At the very top is a massive layer of blocky pink quartzite. This formed near the end

© Michael Burzynski

Cow Head conglomerate records ancient seafloor avalanches.

Graptolite fossil, 5 cm across.

Marine snail fossil.

Trilobite fossil, 20 cm long.

of the Lower Cambrian when mountain-building activity and its consequent erosion poured masses of sand out to sea, burying the limestones.

LIVING IN THE PAST

Laurentia moved to a position just 15° south of the equator, and the tropical warmth was perfect for the formation of large limestone reefs in the marine shallows. At this time there was still almost no life on land, but life flourished in the sea as soft-bodied marine animals were evolving into more complex shelly forms. As they died, hard body parts sank to the seafloor. There they were covered by sediment, preserved from decay, and eventually fossilized.

Rocks laid down during this period contain a record of animal evolution. Organisms in the shallows on either side of the widening Iapetus became separated by greater and greater distances. Eventually there was no interbreeding, and the trilobites, brachiopods, and other organisms began to evolve along different paths.

In the shallows, mats of blue-green algae trapped calcium carbonate from the water, and slowly built up large coral-like mounds. Marine worms crawled over and through the mud, leaving feeding trails and tunnels. As other worm-like animals died, their bodies decomposed except for hard tooth-like parts called conodonts. Sponge "skeletons" littered the sea floor with tiny spicules. Like today's crabs, armour-clad trilobites crept about in myriad shapes and sizes. Above them swam octopus-like cephalopods in conical and coiled shells. Masses of apple-sized snails grazed on the algae. Other snails had long spiral shells like modern whelks. Clam-like brachiopods lived everywhere, with as many shell shapes as there were habitats to fill.

Some of the most abundant animals were graptolites. These colonial animals grew in many different shapes, often resembling branching plants, and they floated near the water surface or lived attached on the seabed. Their remains get their name from the Greek words *graphein* and *lithos*, respectively meaning "to write" and "rock," because these fossils resemble fine pencil marks. Graptolite fossils are tremendously useful to geologists. They were widespread, common, and evolved rapidly. Geologists use the fossils for dating and correlating beds of rock. Finding a particular group of graptolites in a rock is like seeing several cars in an old photograph—they provide a reference, a rough date and location for the formation of the rock.

In a cliff on the western tip of Cow Head peninsula, white limestone boulders a metre or more in diameter are cemented together in a darker matrix of lime mud, thin-bedded limestone, and shale. This coarse Cow Head Conglomerate is known internationally, and it is a record of submarine avalanches along the edge of a reef around 500 million years ago. Storms, earthquakes, or overloading caused the outer edge of the growing reef to fail. Sliding down the shallow slope on a lubricating slurry of silt and water, lumps of shallow-water limestone came to rest in deep water atop fine-layered silt, and were then covered by more layers of silt.

The limestone blocks contain massive algal mounds, trilobite and brachiopod fragments, and cephalopod and snail shells that settled between the

James Steeves, GMNP

Tilted sedimentary rocks at Green Point.

mounds on the reef. The deeper water shales that cover the conglomerate layers contain graptolite fossils. These interlayered rocks give geologists the unusual chance to study organisms in one rock from both shallow water (the light-coloured conglomerate) and oceanic depths (the dark shales). Fossils are often used to age rocks, but since fossils from different environments are rarely found together it is difficult to say whether the organisms lived before, after, or were contemporaneous with those at another site. Finding these deep and shallow-water organisms buried together links them in time.

From the northern boundary of the park to Lobster Cove Head there are remnants of these undersea avalanches. The largest pieces of shallow-water limestone are to the north (Lower Head contains one block 100 metres by 400 metres) and the smallest are to the south. Because large blocks settle faster than small particles, the coarse conglomerates at Cow Head and Lower Head represent portions of avalanches that settled on the ancient continental slope. The conglomerate at Lobster Cove Head and Green Point settled farther downslope.

Interbedded with the limestone and shale are layers and clumps of chert. This rock is composed of silica, mostly from the shells of tiny marine animals. The shells rained down onto the ocean floor, and there hardened into layers of glassy rock. The shells that protected these minute animals were eventually put to another use. Early people along this coast quarried the flint-like chert to fashion knives, harpoon points, and other cutting tools.

The cliffs at Green Point are built of fine layers of dark grey shale—a 30 million year record of sediment accumulation in the depths of Iapetus Ocean. Interlayered with the shales are thicker strata of light-coloured limy sandstone, and some bands of limestone conglomerate. These are a deeper water portion of the same limestone avalanches that occurred at Cow Head. The beds here have been tilted (actually overturned) to an angle of about 115° from the original horizontal sea floor. The rocks to the south are the oldest, and accumulated during the late Cambrian Period. To the north the beds are from the younger Ordovician Period. Each one metre step northward along the cliffs passes about 60,000 years of sediment accumulation.

Hidden in a notch between the Cambrian and Ordovician sediments is the boundary separating those two periods. The fossils here are microscopic, but the record here is so complete and well preserved that the International Union of Geological Sciences is considering Green Point an international standard (or *stratotype*) for defining the boundary between Cambrian and Ordovician.

DEATH OF A GREAT OCEAN, BEDROCK SLIDES INTO PLACE

Amid this explosion of sea life, everything changed. First the drift of continents reversed and the mighty Iapetus ceased to grow, and then the landmasses on either side began moving together. Iapetus got smaller, like today's Pacific, as ocean floor was consumed at subduction zones.

On the boat tour at Trout River Pond, the rocks of the ancient Iapetus Ocean floor are laid bare. Some of these rocks form so deep down that they are rarely seen at the surface of the earth. On the south side of the Pond there are cliffs of grey ocean crust rock. At their top are pillow lavas produced when semi-liquid magma welled out on the sea floor. The cliffs themselves are sheeted dykes of diabase that squeezed up and hardened into new rock below the floor of Iapetus. Below the sheeted dykes (underground) is gabbro, and the fossil mantle. A fault runs down this long lake, and the same gabbro and mantle rock are exposed in the up-faulted rock on the northern shore. The barren ochre-coloured mantle rock of the Tablelands was originally five to ten kilometres below the ocean floor.

This slice of oceanic lithosphere (an *ophiolite*) was forced onto the edge of the sinking western slab as the ocean continued to close. The continental margin of North America bent beneath the advancing ophiolite. Erosion wore away the ophiolite's upper portions, coating the sinking continental margin with sediment. Part of the mystery of the origin of the Tablelands was solved when chromite particles were found in an outcrop of dirty-grey arkosic sandstone at Lobster Cove Head. They could only have come from eroding mantle rock, such as the Tablelands. Since the Tablelands now lies above this sandstone, it must have overridden the arkose as it completed the last part of its voyage.

Ribbon limestones at Lobster Cove Head—part of the mélange.

© Michael Burzynski

Moho rocks, Trout River Pond.

© Michael Burzynski

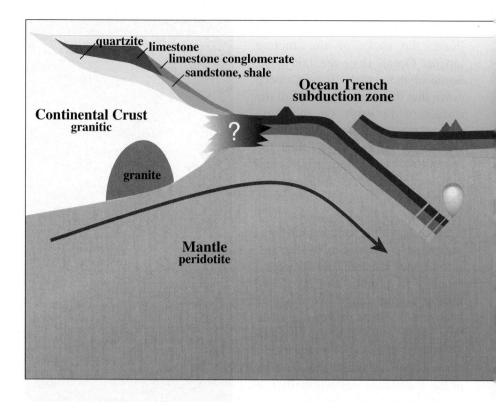

quartzite, limestone
limestone conglomerate
sandstone, shale

Ocean Trench
subduction zone

Continental Crust
granitic

granite

?

Mantle
peridotite

Moho rocks: grey gabbro and brown periodite.

© Michael Burzynski

This key piece of evidence was deduced by geologist Bob Stevens, who along with Hank Williams and other geologists from Memorial University of Newfoundland worked out how the park area's geology was a clear example of the workings of the then-new theory of Plate Tectonics. Discoveries here and elsewhere in Newfoundland were later shown to apply to most of the east coast of North America.

As it moved, the ophiolite scraped up slabs of oceanic rock and continental margin, dragging them along like sticky snow under a toboggan, stacking one atop the other. Underneath, muddy seafloor sediments acted as a lubricant as the ophiolite moved forward. The sediments slipped until water was

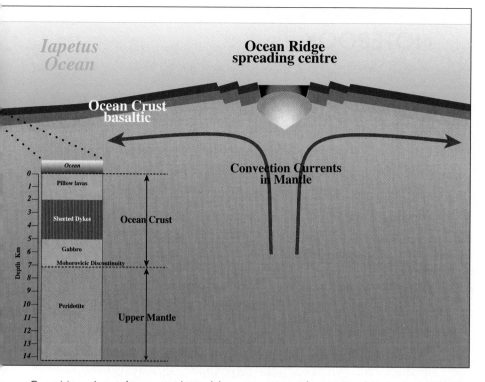

Gros Morne's geology was shaped by movements of tectonic plates around a subduction zone. The depth of the ocean is greatly exaggerated in this diagram. The rocks that comprise an ophiolite suite are derived from oceanic crust and upper mantle.

squeezed out and friction built up. When one layer ceased to lubricate, another began. The shale in dryer layers became crushed and mangled around large blocks of stronger sandstone and limestone. These jumbled and deformed rocks are called *mélange* (French: "a mixture"). Roadcuts in the Rocky Harbour area are full of shattered slates and isolated blocks of limestone and sandstone that range in size from pebbles to hill-sized "knockers" like Lobster Cove Head and Berry Hill.

The sandwich of rock continued to move, bulldozing up and over the deep-water limestone conglomerate, over the reef-like carbonate bank, and over the shallow-water sediments off the North American coast. There it eventually ground to a stop as the Eurafrican and North American continents sidled up together in a slow mountain-raising collision. And there they lay, locked together in a new supercontinent—*Pangaea*.

Down the centre of Pangaea was a mountain chain—the crumpled suture between the original continents. This Caledonide Mountain System was about 4,000 kilometres long, and included today's Appalachians, the Long Range, the Caledonian Mountains in northern Britain, and mountains in Scandinavia. Gros Morne's rocks lay somewhere near the centre, far away

NOTEBOOK

Mohorovicic Discontinuity or *Moho* is a contact zone representing the crust-mantle boundary. Geologists recognize both a seismic Moho (based on composition and density) and a petrologic Moho (based on rock type). The park is one of the first places where it was recognized that "fossil" Moho occurs on land.

Ultramafic rock is dense rock characteristic of the earth's mantle. It is extremely low in silica and high in iron and magnesium. This rock is characteristic of the earth's mantle.

Peridotite is ultramafic rock. There are several forms, all a mix of the minerals olivine and pyroxene together with a range of minor constituents such as chromite.

Serpentinization is the process of chemical alteration of olivines and pyroxenes into serpentinite, usually caused by water circulating within the rock mass. Mantle rock is unstable at the temperatures and pressure of the earth's surface, and alters rapidly in the presence of water and air. The rock serpentinite gets its name from the snakeskin alteration pattern.

Ophiolite suite is a sequence of rocks usually seen where a slice of the sea floor is emplaced on continental crust. This sequence includes ocean floor sediments, oceanic crust rocks such as pillow basalts, sheeted dykes, and gabbro, and rarely the Moho and ultramafic rocks from the earth's mantle. The name is derived from the Greek word *ophis*, meaning "snake," because of the snakeskin pattern often seen on altered peridotite surfaces. The Tablelands is part of the Bay of Islands Ophiolite, which includes the North Arm Massif, the Blow-Me-Down Massif, and the Lewis Hills Massif. Other good examples of ophiolite rocks are found in Cyprus, Oman, Russia, and New Guinea. However, they are more serpentinized, more vegetated, less accessible, or considerably more difficult and dangerous to visit than the Tablelands.

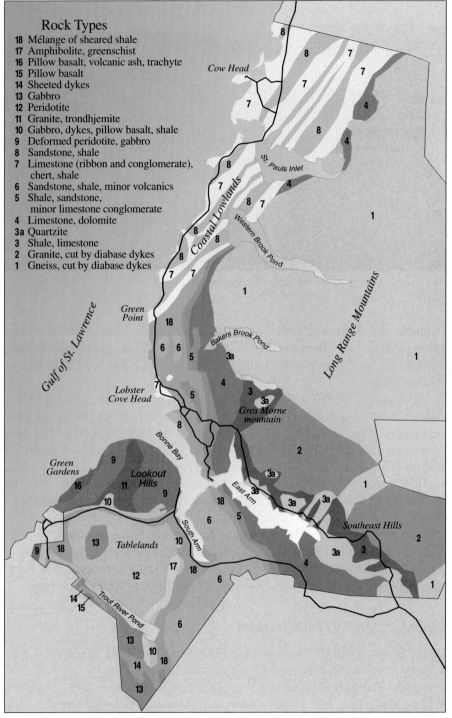

Rock Types

18 Mélange of sheared shale
17 Amphibolite, greenschist
16 Pillow basalt, volcanic ash, trachyte
15 Pillow basalt
14 Sheeted dykes
13 Gabbro
12 Peridotite
11 Granite, trondhjemite
10 Gabbro, dykes, pillow basalt, shale
9 Deformed peridotite, gabbro
8 Sandstone, shale
7 Limestone (ribbon and conglomerate),
   chert, shale
6 Sandstone, shale, minor volcanics
5 Shale, sandstone,
   minor limestone conglomerate
4 Limestone, dolomite
3a Quartzite
3 Shale, limestone
2 Granite, cut by diabase dykes
1 Gneiss, cut by diabase dykes

Simplified Geological Map of Gros Morne National Park. Adapted, with permission, from GSC Miscellaneous Report 54.

The Long Range towers over the coastal lowlands.

from the sea. However, those rocks still contained mementos of their maritime past: the sea floor sediments, the seamount lavas, the marine fossils, and the chunk of ocean crust and upper mantle that is known as the Bay of Islands Ophiolite.

The extinction of part of this ocean is clearly told in the rocks of Gros Morne. It was difficult to decipher, but in the last fifty years geologists have gathered enough data here to read the story of plate tectonics, the most important concept in modern geology. The Tablelands is still the centre of attention for most visiting geologists. At Trout River Pond there is a cross section through the seafloor of Iapetus: down through the crust, past the Mohorovicic Discontinuity, and into the rocks of the mantle itself—a realm normally out of the reach of geologists.

Erosion dismantled the mountains thrown up during continental collision. By 140 million years ago, currents in the mantle were again tugging at Pangaea. The crust pulled apart east of St. John's and a new ocean was born: the Atlantic. It is still growing a couple of centimetres wider each year.

FROM PLAIN TO MOUNTAIN

Along highway 430 between Sally's Cove and Cow Head, the Long Range appears to be a flat-topped wall of forest and rock rising from the coastal lowlands. This raised plateau is the largest and most impressive geological feature in the park. It is part of a peneplain that extends throughout the Cape Breton Highlands and Gaspé Peninsula, and down into Nova Scotia and New Brunswick. By mid to late Tertiary time (between 40 and 50 million years ago), erosion had reduced the east coast of North America to a vast lowland plain with little exposed bedrock. Slow-flowing rivers cut meandering courses through the deep soils of this peneplain.

Movement along a fault lifted a portion of the peneplain about 300 metres some time during the late Tertiary. Encouraged by gravity, erosion sped up, and rejuvenated streams soon cut valleys into softer rock and created a second, lower, erosion plateau. Another lurch upward raised the landscape so that the original peneplain—the top of the Long Range and the Tablelands—lay between 550 and 800 metres above sea level.

ICING THE CAKE

The most popular scenic attractions in today's Gros Morne are the result of one peculiar feature of water: liquid at summer temperatures, water usually turns into solid ice at 0°C. However, under pressure, ice will flow downhill.

About three million years ago the earth's temperature began to fluctuate. During cold periods, snow that fell during one winter did not completely melt away before the next began. Snow banks loitered each summer on north-facing slopes, grew from year to year, and soon there was enough weight to compress the lower snow layers into ice.

When about 20 metres of ice had built up, it began to flow over a lubricating layer of water melted by the pressure above. Inching downhill the juvenile glaciers accumulated bits of rock that scraped the narrow valley walls as they moved. Eventually, huge rivers of ice were scouring their way down to the lowlands through ever-enlarging valleys, lugging loads of excavated sand, gravel, and boulders. Sea level fell throughout the world as water was locked up in ice caps. This was partially countered here by the sinking of Newfoundland under the weight of the accumulating ice.

Since the beginning of the Ice Age, there have been some forty glaciations in the Northern Hemisphere. Each glaciation involved several major periods of ice advance and melt, and each was followed by a warmer interglacial period. Each ice advance scraped into the bedrock, enlarging valleys and steepening their walls—erasing most of the evidence of earlier advances.

Early major glaciations overtopped even the highest hills in the park. One, about 600,000 years ago, scoured across the summits of Gros Morne, Big Hill, the Tablelands, Big Level, and the Rocky Harbour Hills, and left a deposit of loose rock debris called *till*. Weathering has since smoothed the highest parts of this glaciated landscape, turning them into plains of frost-shattered rock rubble called *felsenmeer*.

A more recent glaciation deposited till between 500 and 700 metres above present sea level some 150,000 years ago. It left the park's highest summits unscathed, but lateral moraines mark the upper reach of this ice like a wrack line on the beach. The most recent glaciation started about 85,000 years ago. Its last ice advance was 33,000 years ago, and by 15,000 years ago the ice began to wane. It took another 6,000 years for lingering highland ice to melt in the park area.

Ice formed on several parts of the Island, and in fact the ice that overran the park area came from two sources: one lobe of a large ice cap in the interior of Newfoundland flowed past Deer Lake and out to the Gulf of St. Lawrence through Bonne Bay and a smaller cap on the Long Range Mountains fed ice down through deep troughs (St. Pauls, Western Brook Pond, Bakers Brook Pond, and Ten Mile Pond) onto the coastal lowland and from there to the Gulf.

TRACKS OF THE GLACIERS

From the top of Gros Morne mountain the view takes in the great raised peneplain of the Long Range, and the Ten Mile Pond trough that glaciers carved into it. The Long Range highlands are dissected by these huge glacial valleys, whose cliffs loom over the waters below. Some of these cliffs are 600-metre-high vertical faces that continue far under water. Their sides are stained with minerals and darkened by lichen growth, but in places these cliffs still exhibit the scratches of pebbles that were entrained in the passing ice.

When the ice departed, it left tens of kilometres of cliffs unsupported. But verticality is not a condition that rock finds comfortable, since gravity is constantly trying to pull it down to a more appropriate level. The first stage of the lowering

Jeff Anderson, GMNP

Stress crack atop a cliff in the Long Range.

© Michael Burzynski

Balanced erratic on Old Crow.

Michael Burzynski, GMNP

Lichen-covered felsenmeer on Gros Morne.

process is evident at the cliff edges. They are deeply cracked, and are slowly coming apart along these seams. In some glacial troughs the rock has already slumped. Stress crevasses run along the tops of most of the glacial cliffs in the park, and are particularly clear above Ten Mile Pond and Western Brook Pond.

The signs of middle-age sag are easy to see from below: immense flakes of rock cling precariously to the walls of the cliffs. Overhangs cast dark shadows, and wide scree fans lie piled where rubble has tumbled from the steepest rock faces. Some sheets of cliff are almost bare of lichens, indicating that a slab has cracked free and plunged into the black depths. In geological terms, cliffs are dynamic features. Those rock walls will eventually be down where the water is today.

These troughs vividly indicate the quantity of rock removed by glaciation. They also hint at how much ice flowed down from the Long Range ice caps. Smaller tributary glaciers did not cut as deeply into the rock as the main glaciers, so the mouths of their valleys perch high on the sides of the larger troughs. These U-shaped hanging valleys are responsible for some of the park's waterfalls, and are best seen at St. Pauls Inlet, along Western Brook Pond, and at Burridges Gulch in the Southeast Hills.

Bonne Bay is actually composed of two glacial troughs filled with seawater. They are true fjords. A ridge of rock debris lies in an arc some 20 kilometres off the mouth of the bay. This is the terminal moraine left by Bonne Bay glaciers, and has long been an important fishing bank. One end of this gravelly deposit curves ashore at Sally's Cove.

The highlands were scoured by the ice, and little soil has built up since the last glaciation, so barren rock knobs and rubble fields crown the hills. Rounded boulders, called erratics, litter the landscape, lying as they were dropped when the ice melted. Some are distinct enough to have names such as Sam's Rock and Puncheon Rock, given by the hunters and trappers who

The town of Trout River is built on old delta terraces.

roamed these hills. Other erratics were lowered by the melting ice onto the backs of smaller rocks. Now they teeter or perch daintily with sky showing beneath their bellies, tonnes of boulder standing on delicate stone tiptoes.

Below the summit of Gros Morne, rounded gneiss erratics stand out against the smaller quartzite blocks, like rings on an enormous bathtub. These erratics indicate the highest reach of Long Range ice during the last glaciation. They are traces of two different terminal moraines.

The top of Gros Morne was above the last glaciation, and was probably covered in cold-based ice—ice frozen to the bedrock and unable to move. Parts of the mountain's steep flanks may have been ice free. The deep layer of frost-shattered rock on Gros Morne's summit, and on other peaks along the Long Range, seems to have developed over a much longer period than the last 10,000 ice-free years. This felsenmeer is one of the main clues that led geologists to believe that these peaks are among the parts of Canada that escaped later glaciations. The mountaintop is a good place to visualize the ice filling the great valleys to their brims, slipping towards the coast with its load of rock plucked from the valley walls, then spilling out onto the lowlands as vast flattened lobes that met and forged into the icy sea. Based on the evidence in the rocks, the ice was between 750 and 900 metres deep in the troughs, and had an average depth of 600 metres on the lowlands. When the ice wasted, the

Raised sea cliff near the lighthouse on Cow Head.

Lookout Hills slump.

troughs at Western Brook, Bonne Bay, and Trout River became fjords as seawater flooded inland.

There has been a huge collapse along the northern flank of the Lookout Hills overlooking the mouth of Bonne Bay. The cliffs at the mouth of the bay were both carved and supported by glacier ice, but as the ice wasted away, gravity's call had to be answered. Crevasses rent the length of the clifftop, and slowly parts of the headland separated and sagged downhill in stair-like segments. This is the largest known rock slump in Canada. It is seven kilometres long, up to two kilometres wide, and contains nearly a billion cubic metres of rock that has slid downhill between 50 and 100 metres.

The highest point of the Lookout Hills, Big Lookout, was sliced in half by the sag, and has left a scarp face almost 100 metres high. Several rock pillars along the seaward edge of the slope are also indications of downward slip (they are not raised sea stacks). One of these spires is called "The Old Man" and is clearly visible from Norris Point.

GLACIAL GRAFFITI

On the park lowlands there are huge mounds of bouldery debris between the mouths of Bakers Brook Pond, Western Brook Pond, and St. Pauls Inlet. The rubble was deposited as interlobate moraines between glaciers that swelled outward from the gorges.

Near Gull Rocks lookoff along the East Arm of Bonne Bay there are actual tracks left by glaciers. The long scratches or striae in roadside bedrock were left by rocks dragged along in the moving ice.

The enormous accumulation of ice during glaciations depressed the crust below sea level, allowing the sea to reach higher on the hillsides than it does today. There was greater ice load to the north, so the northern part of the park was pushed even lower than the south; thus relative sea level at St. Pauls Inlet was at 110 metres, compared to 70 metres in the Trout River area.

Melting glaciers spewed gritty water into the sea. Building up over the years, sediment formed thick delta deposits at river mouths. Once the weight of the ice was gone, the land began to rise to its former level. This left the delta deposits high and dry, but with several step-like terraces that record stages in the rebound of the land. Now erosion and man excavate these gravel deltas at Rocky Barachois, Glenburnie, Shoal Brook, and Trout River, exposing the shells of clams and other animals that lived in the glacial sea. At Trout River, the gravels have revealed bird bones, bowhead whale ribs, and even a walrus tusk, all about 12,000 years old.

Trout River and nearby Green Gardens also have other relics of higher sea level. At today's seashore there are sea stacks forming along the cliffs of these two sites. These pillars of rock record how marine erosion has eaten back the cliffs, leaving only remnants standing in the sea, rising from flat intertidal platforms. High above the water, older sea stacks loom over an ancient intertidal platform cut in the bedrock. The fall of sea level marooned these crumbling stone spires, and they now rise out of waving grasses instead of waves. The most accessible raised sea stack in the park area is at Trout River, and is also known as "The Old Man."

Land rose slowly from the sea, exposing near-shore shallows that became the wide coastal lowland at the foot of the Long Range. Sea level change had a serious effect on the fjords at Western Brook and Trout River—cut off from sea by the lowlands, they began to fill with fresh water and became lakes.

Today the sea encroaches on the land—rising at a rate of about 20 centimetres per century, and this rise is estimated to continue for the next thousand years. Coastal erosion is relatively rapid in places, and the sea works its way inland along sections of weak rock or unconsolidated glacial sediments. The slow inland transgression of the sea whittles away at the park bit by bit, but it is also responsible for creating the wild coastal cliffs, the grottos, jutting headlands, crumbling sea stacks, tidepools, small islands, and extensive intertidal platforms.

The sea has always been a barrier to land plants and animals.

ISLAND ARK

EWFOUNDLAND IS AN ISLAND, AND ICE AND WATER have made its plant and animal communities very different from those on the nearby mainland. As glaciers moved down from the hills, melting back time after time, they removed plants and animals, soil, and a good deal of bedrock. When the ice waned, what was left was literally a clean slate. Immigrant plants and animals arrived from elsewhere to recolonize the Island, and the process continues to this day.

ROOTS AND WINGS

All of the species of plants and animals that now live on the Island of Newfoundland have arrived somehow during the last 13,000 years. It is obvious that the 125 kilometres of water between Cape Breton and the Island, or the 18 kilometres that separate Labrador and the tip of the Great Northern Peninsula are not very secure moats.

Peat cores from bogs and fens contain pollen, spores, seeds, and charcoal particles that record the progression of vegetation since the last Ice Age. The story told by these plant sub-fossils suggests that plants began their recolonization of the Island about 12,000 years ago. The first vegetation was like that of today's Arctic tundra, but eventually warmer-climate plants moved in and almost replaced the hardy but slow-growing arctic species. They survived only in marginal habitats: the coastal barrens, serpentine soils, north-facing cliffs, and highland tundra.

© Michael Burzynski

On the Long Range highlands, conditions have changed little since the last glaciation.

Ice-shattered rock, still barren after 10,000 years, covers much of the highlands.

Plants with tiny spores or seeds probably blew over from the mainland, and even some of the larger-seeded trees such as spruce, pine, and fir could have arrived during exceptional storms. Other seeds floated across, then washed up on beaches and were blown inland to fertile soil. Plants with edible berries were probably deposited on the island as seeds encased in a little dollop of natural manure when birds flying from the mainland excreted spent fuel. Most insects fly, and young spiders often "balloon" for tens of kilometres with drogue lines of silk. Most birds also got here by air. However, floating, flying, and fertilizer cannot explain the origin of all of the plants and animals found on the Island. Another problem is that some plants and animals have extraordinary disjunct ranges—they are separated by hundreds or thousands of kilometres from their closest relatives in the Arctic, the western (Cordilleran) mountains, or in Eurasia.

The Québec botanist-monk Frère Marie-Victorin proposed several hypotheses to explain the peculiar distribution of plants around the Gulf of St. Lawrence. Arctic plants on the Island can be explained by imagining what it may have been like as the ice front melted northward at the end of the last glaciation. Plants would colonize the newly exposed moist gravels almost as quickly as the ice melted back. Plants able to live closest to the ice would be those already adapted to a short cool growing season. As the ice retreated, these plants continued to flourish in the periglacial conditions at the melting ice edge, but they were replaced by more vigorous boreal plants as the ice withdrew from an area. Small numbers of these plants were able to survive on the Island on cold mountain tops, exposed coastal cliffs, and difficult serpentine or limestone soils, while their relatives retreated farther and farther northward with the glaciers.

Hiking on the Long Range highlands.

The many disjunct Cordilleran and Eurasian plants are a bit more difficult to explain. Perhaps one or two species did arrive as wind- or bird-borne seeds, but that still entails a journey of thousands of kilometres. Instead of invoking the unreasonable odds necessary for this to occur, botanists have suggested that these plants were originally more widespread. During the last glaciation, some species of plants and animals probably survived on coastal or mountaintop refuges on the Island, and perhaps on the Grand Banks and other offshore shallows which would have been exposed as dry land by the lower sea levels. These refuges then served as sources for the repopulation of the Island after glaciation.

The famous Harvard University field-botanist Merritt Lyndon Fernald (1873-1950) climbed many of the highlands on the west coast between 1911 and 1929, identifying numerous endemic species and subspecies. He was struck by the similarities between plant communities on highlands throughout the Gulf of St. Lawrence region, and by what he interpreted as the absence of recent glaciation on the highest hills. Although his postulated refuges are still being debated by both botanists and geologists, the disjunct plants remain a key feature of the flora of Newfoundland's west coast.

Gros Morne's complicated geological history has left it with many different bedrock types and associated soils. The resulting topography rears from sea level to 800-metre-high hilltops. Growing conditions range from mild and sheltered to subarctic. This creates a wide variety of habitats, and so far 725 species of vascular plants have been identified within the park, and there are many more hundreds of lichens, fungi, mosses, and liverworts.

ANIMALS ON THE ROCK

Most visitors notice that Newfoundland has far fewer roadkills than the mainland. Although this is bad news for crows, ravens, and foxes, it is one of the advantages of driving on the Island. The disadvantage is that when you do hit an animal on a Newfoundland road, it is more than likely to be a moose. This lack of small curb-side carrion is another result of Newfoundland's isolation from the mainland, and is again due to the water barrier.

Seawater is a difficult obstacle for animals to overcome. Many mainland animals have never made it to the Island (there are no striped skunks in Newfoundland, nor are there freshwater turtles, tortoises, snakes, newts, salamanders, groundhogs, raccoons, porcupines, bobcats, lemmings, moles, fishers, wolverines, jumping mice, flying squirrels, grey squirrels, or white-tailed deer). There are no native shrews, toads, frogs, ruffed grouse, spruce grouse, deer mice (or any other kind of mice), snowshoe hares, mink, moose, chipmunks, or red squirrels—all residents of the nearby mainland that have been introduced to the Island accidentally or on purpose in the last few generations.

True native species, such as caribou, red foxes, lynx, and timber wolves, probably walked to the Island over the ice in winter, as the coyote did recently from Nova Scotia. It is harder to imagine how some other species made it. Black bears, for example, sleep through much of the winter, but may have crossed on the ice. Another possibility is that they too survived the glaciation in offshore refuges, and then repopulated the Island once the ice melted.

Newfoundland's fauna, like its flora, is a peculiar mix of immigrants that have found ways of getting here and then surviving with each other on this harsh but spectacular isle. Mammals show the greatest effect of this watery filter. Fifteen species are native to the Island. In contrast, nearby

Different animals colonized the Island in different ways.

Labrador has 34 species of mammals, and Cape Breton Island has 39. Of Newfoundland's native fifteen, seven were predators, two were insect eaters, and only five were plant eaters. This carnivore to herbivore ratio is completely reversed from the usual condition on the mainland.

After thousands of years of isolation from their mainland relatives, nine species of Newfoundland mammals are distinct enough to be classified as subspecies. The fast rate of species development on the Island, essentially the evolution of differences between mainland and Island populations, could be due to the restricted gene pool of island mammals, but it could also reflect the adaptation of Island mammals to the wide range of habitats available because of lack of competition. Gros Morne contains such a wide range of habitats that all of the original mammals of the Island were native here. Most of the introduced species have also found their way to the park.

Newfoundland Timber Wolf—originally roamed the entire Island. Woodland Caribou were its major prey, mainly because the only other menu items were Arctic hares, meadow voles, Newfoundland beavers, Newfoundland muskrats, birds, and smaller carnivores.

As everywhere else in their range, wolves were considered to be worth far more dead than alive. Newfoundland declared a bounty on wolves in 1839, and bounty hunting and fur trapping doomed what had probably always been a small

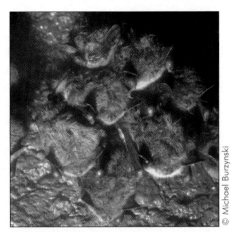
Little brown bats.

Newfoundland meadow vole.

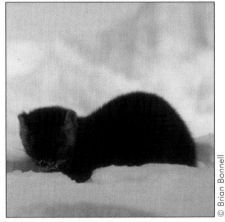
Newfoundland marten.

population. By 1863 the bounty was suspended, indicating that the wolf population had already been drastically reduced. The last wolf killed on the Island was taken near Daniel's Harbour around 1920. Although there were several sightings in the early 1920s, whatever animals survived could not maintain a viable population. Having completed its work with pitiless efficiency, Newfoundland's *Act to Encourage the Killing of Wolves* was finally repealed in 1963. All that remains of the Newfoundland timber wolf are stories, a few bones, and one mounted skin. Many believe that timber wolves will eventually colonize the Island from Labrador.

Newfoundland Red Fox—native to the Island of Newfoundland, with a great natural diversity in markings and fur colour that was noted as far back as 1870. Many of the park foxes are almost black or silvery. Foxes are omnivores, taking advantage of all available small game, carrion, insects, berries, seeds, and vegetation. They use smelly droppings and urine as scent markings to define territories. The introduction of moose and snowshoe hare to the Island has probably greatly increased fox populations, since foxes frequently scavenge carrion from large animal carcasses, especially in winter. The fox population in the park is high, so it is lucky that rabies is not prevalent on the Island.

© Michael Burzynski

Newfoundland red fox.

Some foxes have learned to beg for food along roadsides. This presents a traffic hazard, and also puts people who illegally feed the foxes at risk of bites or parasites. Foxes that lose their wariness of people and vehicles in this way usually end up as traffic fatalities.

Newfoundland Black Bear—the Island subspecies has one of the longest hibernation periods of any bear in North America. It is also thought to be among the largest of black bears, and perhaps the most carnivorous since a large part of their diet comes from scavenged or fresh big game. The greatest recorded weight for a Newfoundland black bear is 240 kilograms, though the average weight of a male is 180 kilograms. Dozens of bears regularly use the park for browsing, hunting, and denning.

Philippe Henry, GMNP

Newfoundland black bear with radio collar.

It is not uncommon to come across bear tracks and droppings in the park, but it very rare to see a bear, except at a great distance. They are often seen foraging for berries on the highland and lowland barrens in autumn. For the most part, bears' greatest interest in humans is in avoiding us. Bears are at the very top of the food chain on this Island. Hikers and campers are part way down that chain. Once accustomed to human food and the smell of people, bears start to regard us less as a threat and more as a meal ticket. Dump bears and bears that scavenge around messy campsites can get aggressive. To avoid this, and the consequent killing of problem bears, the park insists that all campers and hikers follow proper procedures in bear country. Please ask for bear information at the Visitor Centre as soon as you arrive.

Newfoundland Lynx—short-tailed wildcats that originally preyed on caribou calves, beavers, muskrats, Arctic hares, and ground-nesting birds. Lynx were so uncommon that many writers in the last century considered them only occasional visitors from Labrador. After the introduction of snowshoe hares in the mid-1800s the lynx population increased dramatically. It has been estimated that a lynx can eat as many as 200 hares per year. Lynx numbers mirror the highs and lows of the snowshoe hare cycles across the Island.

Newfoundland Marten (*sable* or *marten-cats*)—trapped by the tens of thousands for export to Europe

Newfoundland lynx.

© Dennis Minty

Short-tailed weasel.

© Michael Burzynski

Newfoundland beaver.

© Michael Burzynski

Woodland caribou on a snowbed in the Long Range.

and almost extirpated by the beginning of the twentieth century. They are now an endangered subspecies. Marten numbers plummetted from over-hunting and habitat destruction, and although protected on the Island since 1934, marten numbers have not recovered. Marten require mature conifer-ous forest with lots of fallen trunks that they use for travelling and denning. **Newfoundland Short-tailed Weasel** (*ermine*)—small but voracious preda-tors, they will tackle prey many times larger than themselves. The coat is reddish brown in summer, except for the black tip of the tail. Movements are fast and almost snakelike. Sometimes weasels are seen running across a road with prey in mouth, head and tail held high. In winter their coat is white, and only the large black eyes and black tail tip stand out. Weasels, like most musteline, have musk glands near the anus. When scared or when marking territory they secrete some of the pasty musk, releasing a smell that is very similar to that of their relative the skunk.

Newfoundland River Otter—a small dark subspecies that is at home in salt water and fresh. Otters are seen swimming near shore in Bonne Bay, and in the ponds of the lowlands. They feed mainly on fish, but will take small mammals, nestling birds, marine invertebrates, insects, and many other kinds of food. They are wonderful swimmers and their smooth dives and antics in the water make them look like a cross between a seal and a snake.

Newfoundland Woodland Caribou—the only ungulate native to the Island of Newfoundland (and the source of names such as Deer Lake and Deer

Arm). The province has the largest and healthiest herd of woodland caribou in the world, with an estimated population of 70,000 animals on the Island alone. Of that, about 2,000 caribou live in and around Gros Morne National Park.

Woodland caribou are much smaller than moose. A fully grown adult male can weigh up to 270 kilograms, and females are about a quarter smaller. Unlike any other ungulates (except the closely related reindeer), both male and female caribou can grow antlers. Females' antlers are smaller and often point straight backward, while those of the males get larger and more ornate as the animals reach their prime. Stag antlers curve strongly forward and have special flattened tines protecting the forehead, one usually larger than the other. Right and left antlers on the same animal usually look very different.

Stags start to grow their antlers in April, and the velvet is rubbed off in mid-October when the females become sexually receptive. After the rut, between mid-November and late December, most stags shed their antlers. Pregnant does keep their spiky antlers throughout the winter and lose them only after the birth of their calves. During the winter caribou spend most of their time in the open. Their light-brown winter coats bleach almost white in the sun. As winter ends they move up onto the highlands again to reach the calving grounds.

© Michael Burzynski

It is sometimes difficult for caribou to find enough breeze to keep flies away.

Females have their young in June. They then gravitate towards the long-lasting snowbeds that cling to the northern slopes of hills around Big Level. Sometimes two hundred or more animals will cluster on a snowbed. Usually a doe has a single calf, very rarely twins. Calves are cream coloured at birth, but later they grow darker coats and develop a line of faint spots on their haunches. Although wobbly legged at first, they are able to travel with their mothers just hours after birth, and quickly become fast runners. A calf stays with its mother for a full year, and leaves only as she readies to give birth again.

Since the autumn of 1991, caribou have wintered in large numbers on the lowland bogs north of Lobster Cove Head. Between 800 and 1,000 caribou feed and rest on the open bogs each winter. They move about in herds of ten to a hundred animals, feeding on the bogs and picking through the seaweed mulch and leftover vegetables in roadside gardens, but when icy crust covers the bogs they split into much smaller herds and move into the forest to feed on tree lichen. Because caribou live in herds and moose are usually seen alone, most people think that there are far more caribou in the park than moose. Actually there are about five moose to each caribou.

Caribou and their movements have been studied intensively in the park.

Michael Burzynski, GMNP

Autumn migration to the lowlands seems to be a traditional pattern for caribou in the park area, and was noted in the 1860s. In the early 1900s caribou abandoned the lowlands and stayed on the highlands throughout the winter. This may have been due to the increasing hunting pressure, or part of a long-term cyclic change based on the availability of winter food. Perhaps now the highland lichen are depleted, and caribou undertake this short migration to find new feeding grounds. Caribou can smell the lichen that they eat through fifty centimetres or more of snow, and leave a cratered landscape as they paw through the crust to reach them.

Originally, the wolf was the most important predator of caribou

Caribou stags spar frequently in the autumn.

herds, but now bears and lynx fill that role, and even predatory birds may take small weak calves on occasion.

A running caribou picks up its feet like a trained trotter. Head high, nose raised, the high stepping, toe flicking run of a caribou looks bouncy and limber from the side, but from behind it is more comical. Caribou bottoms wobble in retreat—these animals do a wet-diaper waddle that completely belies their usual grace.

Newfoundland Arctic Hare—for many years a symbol for Gros Morne National Park. Some of the initial impetus for setting aside a park was to protect an Arctic hare population on the Island.

Although big (up to 6 kilograms), Arctic hares in Newfoundland are the southernmost in the world, and have the lowest reproductive potential of any hare or rabbit in the world—one litter per year with an average of three young. In the exposed environment of the Long Range hilltops, the leverets must contend with predation by foxes, lynx, hawks, and owls, and with changeable and extreme weather conditions. The actual number of Arctic hares in the park is unknown, but it may be less than a hundred. The best place to see them is atop Gros Morne mountain.

Arctic hares are white in winter (except for eyes and ear tips), but their coat becomes mottled grey in summer and blends in perfectly with the rocks and lichen. They prefer the boulder fields of treeless tundra barrens, and stay

Daniel Boisclair, GMNP

Roger Eddy, GMNP

Arctic hare, summer pelage.　　　　　Arctic hare, winter pelage.

there even in the depths of winter. Unlike populations in the Arctic, Newfoundland hares do not stand on their hind legs to watch for predators, nor do they bounce off at high speed like kangaroos, or even form large herds.

Favourite foods are dwarf willows, birches, alders, heaths, and the leaves and twigs of berry plants. In spring, hares' mouths are stained brown with the resins from munched willow buds. In winter, they use their long claws to dig through packed snow, and their long forward-pointing incisors to clip out twigs. They will also eat carrion if they find it, and gnaw bones and antlers for calcium and phosphorus.

Arctic hares recycle their own night faeces each morning. This runs the vegetable matter through their digestive tract a second time, and nutrients and vitamins can be more efficiently absorbed. Coprophagy is an important adaptation to the impoverished conditions of the barrens, especially in winter. The Arctic hare remains one of the rarest animals in the park, a survivor from the time when the last glaciation was waning and tundra covered the entire area.

Newfoundland Beaver—the Newfoundland subspecies is considered to be slightly darker and smaller than its mainland cousins. By the early part of the 1900s, beavers had been almost eradicated from the Island by relentless trapping. Restocking from the few remaining colonies between 1930 and 1950 restored the population, and now signs of beavers' tree cutting, lodge construction, canals, and dams are visible in many waterways in the park.

Beavers will explore and attempt to use and modify almost any available habitat. They have built in the middle of a wide bog near St. Pauls, they venture into salt water in the East Arm, and even attempt to live on the highlands. They tend to be most active at dawn and dusk. Favourite foods are the underwater stems of yellow pondlily, alder branches, birch, poplar, and raspberry. No matter what some woodsmen insist, beavers do not eat fish. **Newfoundland Muskrat**—originally common in the lowland wetlands, muskrats have been almost eradicated by the introduced mink. Muskrats spend most of their lives in and around water, and feed mainly on streamside plants, insects, and freshwater clams. They dig bank dens along the edges of marshes, or build metre-high piles of vegetation that resemble small beaver lodges. There they overwinter and bear their young. Muskrats are much smaller than beavers, and their long tails are flattened along the sides. An eel-like sculling of this tail propels the muskrat through the water. **Newfoundland Meadow Vole**—the only native small rodent, they are found throughout the Island in lowland sedge fens and meadows. Since there is no competition from other voles they have adapted to exploit most habitats to some extent and have been seen on top of the Tablelands and the Long Range. In spring the winter tunnels of meadow voles melt out of the snow, leaving serpentine trails of packed grass lying on the surface of the ground. **Little Brown Bat**—tiny night acrobats that feed on insects, bats are often seen along streams, trails, and roads at dusk. They roost during the day in hollow trees, under the eaves of houses, in rock crevices, and in caves. Watch for them around buildings and streetlights as they hunt for moths. Gros Morne lies within the range of the eastern long-eared bat (Keen's bat), but this small dark-brown bat has not yet been confirmed here.

INTRODUCED SPECIES

Unfortunately, there is a long history of people releasing foreign animals and plants on the Island of Newfoundland. Each of these introductions has altered the ecology of the Island. The natural communities that have evolved here since the last glaciation have been forced to accommodate the new plants and animals, and each time something special about the Island has been lost. The Island is gradually becoming more and more like the mainland, and less like the Newfoundland of the past.

Most of the animals successfully introduced to the Island are now found in Gros Morne National Park. None of these species was here 150 years ago, and their invasion of the forests, wetlands, and barrens has permanently altered these ecosystems. It is noteworthy that four of the most abundant mammals on the Island today are introduced species: snowshoe hare, moose, red squirrel, and masked shrew. **Masked Shrew**—33 of these small, grey, insect-eating mammals were released on the Island in 1958 as a biological control for the larch sawfly. No shrews of any species lived on the Island before then, and the introduction reduced the numbers of sawflies, and many other insects as well. The word hyperactivity was probably coined to describe something like the masked shrew. They power their way through life in overdrive, and are able to produce several broods of young each year. Now they are found throughout the Island.

Tiny shrews are often seen rushing across roads, looking like bumblebees on roller skates. Even though they are numerous, masked shrews are small and secretive. Domestic cats catch large numbers around communities, and because they are so small, even robins have been seen to eat them. They hunt for small prey such as grubs, spiders, ants, and woodlice (locally called *carpenters*). They climb well and are so light that they can drop from trees with impunity.

In winter, shrews live mostly under the snow, climbing to the surface where a twig has melted a hole in the snow. From there they burrow in the loose flakes just below the snow surface. Their tunnels look like a length of quarter-inch rope covered with snow. Rarely do shrews run across the surface of the snow, and when they do their tiny paired tracks barely leave a mark.

Snowshoe Hare—introduced to the Island between 1864 and 1876 from Nova Scotia to provide meat for outport settlements that were almost completely isolated from other supplies during the winter. The hares have certainly lived up to their end of the bargain. Even today many Newfoundlanders snare them during the winter, and on a pound for pound basis the hunt produces even more wild meat for the Island than moose and caribou combined. Snowshoe hares get their name for their wide hind paws. They can produce two to four litters each summer, with an average of four leverets per litter. Brown in summer, they turn white in winter.

In the Rocky Harbour area in spring, snowshoe hares graze on outcrops of yellowish dolomite in the woods. Each ridge of rock protruding above the snow bears tooth marks, and in places a centimetre or more of stone has been removed. Probably the hares are supplementing

Masked shrew.

© Michael Burzynski

Snowshoe hare.

© Michael Burzynski

their diet with extra calcium and perhaps magnesium. Certainly lithophagy sharpens their rapidly growing incisors—whetting their teeth as they whet their appetites. Hares will also gnaw on shed antlers and the bones of dead animals—digesting the apatite from other animals' bones to obtain calcium and phosphorus for their own—a true appetite for apatite.

Deer Mouse

Red Squirrel—the first unauthorized introduction was in 1963 when a few animals from Labrador were released near Roddickton, north of the park. Red squirrels were first recorded in Gros Morne in 1976. Now they are found everywhere that there are trees, even on the highlands. Squirrels feed mainly on vegetation, berries, fungi, and tree seeds. Each squirrel has preferred feeding sites, and the ground around these stumps and boulders is often covered with middens of empties—cones chewed apart to reach the nutritious seeds inside. Squirrels have also been seen to eat small birds, including fledged robins. Their presence in the forests of the Island may reduce the number of cones available to crossbills and other seed-eating birds, and may even diminish the reproductive potential of trees such as white pine. They have also been seen to feed on the flowers and seeds of such uncommon plants as yellow mountain-saxifrage.

House Mouse and Norway Rat—these lovers of humans and their towns are found in small numbers around communities.

Deer Mouse—first seen in the park in 1995, these small forest rodents were most likely introduced from the mainland in bales of hay. They will probably increase rapidly, but their effect on native plants, spiders, and insects remains to be seen.

North American Moose—ranks a close second to cod in the hearts and passions of many Newfoundlanders. There is no legal hunting in the park, so the moose population is large and serves as a reservoir for stocking the surrounding area.

Moose were introduced to the Island in 1878 and 1904. The first release was only two animals, and probably failed. The second consisted of two cows and two bulls. From that tiny gene pool grew the healthy population of the entire Island. Moose seem to have reached the Gros Morne area by 1925, and were common by the late 1940s.

In 1998 the park moose population was estimated at 8,500 animals. This is one of the highest densities recorded in the world. Moose on the Island feed primarily on balsam fir. At present the park moose population

© Philippe Henry

Bull moose with partially-grown rack still in velvet.

is so large that they are depleting young hardwoods and even retarding the regeneration of balsam fir. In winter they prefer south-facing slopes, which are warmer and usually covered with white birch and balsam fir. Throughout the park it is easy to find stunted firs and other trees whose branches have been chewed down to nubs, and others that have died from overbrowsing.

The best time to see moose in the park is along the roads from late May to early June, usually in the morning or evening. If you encounter a moose on the road while driving, pull over for a few minutes and give the animal enough time to find its way back into the forest—do not try to pass it with your car. There is an average of one moose-vehicle accident per day on the Island of Newfoundland, resulting in ten to twelve human deaths each year. The only safe way to drive in moose country is below the speed limit.

Mink—brought to the Island for fur farming in the 1930s. Escaped animals have now inhabited most of the Island. The first mink was trapped in the park area in 1966. Primarily because of predation by mink, the Newfoundland muskrat has become rare. Many ground-nesting birds probably also suffer from predation, although mink spend most of their time along rivers and the coast where they hunt for fish, small mammals, and invertebrates.

Eastern coyote, a new mammal on the Island.

© Michael Burzynski

VISITORS AND SETTLERS

Polar Bear—although there are no recent records of polar bears in the park, they have been relatively frequent accidental visitors in the past. Naturalist Henry Reeks wrote in 1870 about two polar bears that lived for an entire summer on the Cow Head peninsula. The annual polar bear is usually seen somewhere on the Island in April. It is quickly trapped, tranquilized, and transported back to Labrador.

Eastern Coyote—in the late 1980s, ferry passengers crossing between Cape Breton and Newfoundland watched a small pack of coyotes make its way across the ice from Cape Breton. Another pack was seen trotting ashore near Stephenville. These intelligent and remarkably adaptable animals have spread throughout the Island, including Gros Morne.

Coyotes eat a wide variety of foods including carrion, seeds, berries, vegetation, eggs, insects, and pretty well anything else that can be digested. They earn the dislike of humans by occasionally eating sheep, cats, and the odd crackie (a *crackie* is a small dog of uncertain pedigree, and most crackies are odd to the point of being inedible).

Arctic Fox—occasional visitor from the north. They drift down on ice pans and sometimes come ashore in the park area. They are not known to breed on the Island. One was seen in Norris Point in April 1997.

AMPHIBIANS AND REPTILES

This is a short section: there are no native amphibians on the Island of Newfoundland. Green frogs and common toads have been introduced. Toads are common in some places around Wiltondale, and green frogs live in many park ponds and lakes.

There are also no native terrestrial reptiles in Gros Morne. The park is, however, occasionally visited by marine turtles. The only species reported is the massive leatherback turtle—a connoisseur of jellyfish. These are the largest of living turtles, with shells up to 1.75 metres long. About every five years there is a sighting along the park coast. The most recent leatherback turtle was seen on the beach in Rocky Harbour in the autumn of 1995, and a pair stayed for about two weeks in the Rocky Harbour area in 1990.

FRESHWATER FISH

Even the waters of Newfoundland are different from the mainland. Only seven species and one subspecies of fish are known to breed in the inland waters of Gros Morne, and they are all species that usually spend part of their lives in salt water: speckled trout, Atlantic salmon, Arctic char (and pygmy Arctic char), rainbow smelt, threespine stickleback, ninespine stickleback, and common eels. Four other species—rainbow trout, fourspine stickleback, black-spotted stickleback, and tomcod—have been found in the park, but it is not known whether they breed here.

Atlantic Salmon—one of the most important reasons for settlement along this coast, commercial fishing for Atlantic salmon lasted here until 1992. Largest of the fish found in freshwater, Atlantic salmon spend their first few years growing in brooks before swimming to sea for one to three years and returning as grilse, or sexually mature adults. They are found in all of the major watersheds in the park, and nonmigratory, or landlocked salmon called *ouananiche* live in Wigwam Pond. Nine rivers in Gros Morne either now support Atlantic salmon stocks, or once did, and there are few other places in the world where there are such rivers within a protected park.

In some highland lakes there are landlocked salmon that are severely dwarfed by their living conditions. They reached the ponds during a period of higher sea level and greater river flow. Long isolated by waterfalls, any fish that swam downstream from these lakes could never return, so the trait of seaward migration was lost from highland fish populations. Highland ouananiche grow slowly in their cold, nutrient-poor lakes—reaching a maximum length of only 25 centimetres. They produce only a tiny fraction of the eggs that a regular salmon can lay, so their reproductive rate is very low. They also look like juveniles even when mature. Water insects and other aquatic animals are their major food, not fish like the large anadromous salmon eat.

Atlantic salmon return to freshwater to spawn.

Speckled Trout—(*brook* or *mud trout*) the fish that spring trouting fever is all about. Beautifully coloured, they are still fairly common in most streams, and some run to sea to feed and return as large silvery "sea trout." All park rivers and most large streams support runs of sea trout.

Arctic Char—populations in the park are now all landlocked (nonanadromous) fish. They live in Western Brook Pond, Western Brook, Wigwam Pond, Deer Arm Pond, and perhaps Bakers Brook Pond. A pygmy subspecies is restricted to a few highland lakes in the Upper Humber drainage.

Pygmy Arctic char that live in Hardings Pond on the highlands rarely exceed a length of 15 centimetres. They are considered to be a relict form, surviving there since the last glaciation. They grow slowly, produce few eggs, retain parr marks as adults, and do not show the usual male-female differences at maturity. They are very different from char that live in lowland lakes and in lower portions of the Humber River. As with the dwarfed salmon, it is probably long isolation, acidic water conditions, and the scarcity of food that have led to these differences.

Some anglers propose to alter the barriers outside the park that stop lowland fish from moving upstream, or to introduce fingerlings of the larger fish to upper parts of the Humber River. This would compromise the genetic isolation of the small highland fish, and could lead to their extirpation through disease, competition, or predation.

Rainbow Smelt—most commonly found in Rocky Harbour Pond, Trout River Pond, Western Brook, Wigwam Pond, Lomond River, and East Branch Lomond River. They probably also run into other lakes and rivers in the park. There is a small winter ice fishery for smelt along this coast.

Common Eel—most lowland streams, lakes, and ponds harbour eels, but there are none on the highlands. On occasion, pencil-sized juvenile eels writhe and slither across lowland bogs as they move from one pond to another.

Threespine Stickleback—it is not uncommon to see colourful male Threespine sticklebacks guarding their nests and fending off other males and other fish in the shallows of the lower Lomond River. They are also frequent members of the tidepool fauna, and school in estuarine shallows. These small fish are an important prey species for salmon and large trout, as well as for fish-eating birds. Fourspine, ninespine, and black-spotted sticklebacks are very uncommon in the park, and outside their usual range.

Adult and caterpillar of the Newfoundland short-tailed swallowtail. Insects and other invertebrates also help to illustrate the story of recolonization of the Island.

BIRDS

Birds are not so easily foiled by a marine barrier. So far, 236 species of birds have been seen in Gros Morne, about seventy percent of the more than 335 that have been recorded for the Island of Newfoundland. So far, 101 of Gros Morne's bird species are confirmed as nesting in the park, and 27 more are probable or possible nesters. This reflects the high proportion of vagrants on the Newfoundland bird list—birds that are blown in from all around the compass by storms.

Breeding Species—the most common breeding species in Gros Morne, in rough decreasing order of abundance, are: blackpoll warbler, magnolia warbler, white-throated sparrow, northern waterthrush, yellow-bellied fly-catcher, Lincoln's sparrow, ruby-crowned kinglet, fox sparrow, yellow-rumped warbler, robin, hermit thrush, Swainson's thrush, grey-cheeked thrush, mourning warbler, black-throated green warbler, and yellow warbler.

Birds of Interest—the most asked about birds in the park are: willow ptarmigan, rock ptarmigan, black-backed woodpecker, boreal owl, boreal chickadee, white-winged crossbill, mourning warbler, white-rumped sandpiper, black-headed gull, and dovekie. For recent locations, see the *Sightings Book* at the Visitor Centre.

Pelagic Birds—only the black guillemot breeds in the park area. Occasional visitors include: northern fulmar, greater shearwater, sooty shearwater, manx shearwater, Wilson's storm-petrel, Leach's storm-petrel, northern gannet, pomarine jaeger, parasitic jaeger, long-tailed jaeger, and black-legged kittiwake.

Seabirds—because it lacks large cliffy islands, Gros Morne has no colonies of seabirds such as murres, puffins, razorbills, and gannets—although small numbers of these birds are seen on occasion. Black guillemots nest on islands and cliffs in the park area, especially south of Trout River. Arctic terns and common terns nest on several islands in the St. Pauls-Cow Head area. Stearin Island was named for them, but in the last decade they have been displaced by greater black-backed gulls and herring gulls. The name *Stearing Island* shows up on Captain James Cook's 1768 map of this coast, and comes from the old name for tern (*S t e a r i n*), still used in Newfoundland. This is similar to the French name *sterne* and the Latin name *sterna*. Gull and tern eggs were once an important source of fresh food for isolated communities.

Male black-backed woodpecker at nest hole.
© Michael Burzynski

Black-capped chickadee.
© Michael Burzynski

Boreal chickadee.
© Michael Burzynski

Grey jay in autumn larch.

Female pine grosbeak in mountain ash.

Snowy owls are occasional visitors.

Double-crested cormorants (known as *shags*) are occasional visitors; Shag Cliff, opposite Norris Point is named after them.

Harlequin Duck—colourful birds that nest along fast-flowing highland streams. Their ducklings feed on stream insects, including the larvae and pupae of blackflies. From a purely selfish point of view, anyone who spends time in the backcountry should hope for a dramatic increase in harlequin duck numbers. In the 1860s, naturalist Henry Reeks reported the harlequin duck to be "A common summer migrant, and breeds on the borders of lakes and rivers flowing into the sea, frequently many miles in the country, whence it brings its young in July. The male of this species, which is called a 'lord' in Newfoundland, is decidedly the handsomest little duck inhabiting those cold regions, and is a most expert diver."

These small colourful *lords and ladies* were common enough that a cove in the East Arm of Bonne Bay was named after them. The eastern North American population is now considered endangered. Family groups are occasionally seen along Western Brook. Any sightings would be appreciated by the park, since there are fewer than 1,000 of them left in eastern North America.

Merlin—the most common breeding raptor in the park, this small hawk is easily seen in spring and fall.

Northern Harrier and Short-eared Owl—both species patrol the park's lowland bogs and meadows, the harrier in daylight and the owl as the light grows dim. Both use hearing as well as sight to hunt for meadow voles and other small mammals, gliding low over the ground and occasionally hovering.

Willow Ptarmigan and Rock Ptarmigan—these two species of ptarmigan rarely live in the same habitat, but Gros Morne is one of the few places in their range where they come into frequent contact. It is not unusual to see both species within a couple of hundred metres on the summit of Gros Morne mountain, and sometimes in the autumn they feed in mixed groups.

Harlequin ducks, an endangered species.

Rock ptarmigan are probably the only true Arctic birds. They breed in the Arctic and live there throughout the year, not migrating as do most birds. They are found throughout the Arctic, and are almost completely restricted to it, with only a few outlier populations—such as on the Long Range. They are beautifully adapted to life in a harsh cold environment. Rock ptarmigan differ from willow ptarmigan in several ways: rock ptarmigan are smaller, the Newfoundland subspecies tends to be grey in summer instead of rusty brown, and in winter the males and most females have a distinct black eye stripe.

Willow ptarmigan.

Newfoundland rock ptarmigan are considered to be a separate subspecies from other rock ptarmigan in the world. It is also thought that they are extremely rare. There may be fewer than a thousand of them alive, and they inhabit only a handful of highlands on the Island. One of their main population centres is the Long Range in the park area. Winter

Rock ptarmigan.

food is scarce, and the cold season lasts a long time, so these birds have become expert at conserving precious energy. Usually they depend on camouflage for protection, and do not fly unless badly frightened. Flight takes a lot of energy. This is especially true in winter, and it is thought that as few as one or two flights in winter may be enough to exhaust them, resulting in death.

Both species feed mainly on the buds, leaves, and berries of shrubs. Willow ptarmigan usually live and feed in hardwood stands on hillsides and along rivers, and dangle from the branches of willows, alders, and birches as they reach for food. Drivers often mistake ptarmigan in roadside trees for lumps of snow or wind-blown plastic shopping bags. Rock ptarmigan have a harder time reaching their winter food. They must peck and scratch through hard-packed snow, or find places where snow has blown away from twigs. Because of the fibrous nature of their food, ptarmigan droppings seem to be composed of sawdust, and look like a small pile of cigarette butts (the white "filter" on fresh droppings is uric acid crystals—birds do not excrete liquid urine).

Autumn is the time to see large numbers of these birds in one place. Young of the summer are still together with the adults, and some family groups amalgamate. Half a dozen to two dozen birds will feed in a flock, moving slowly through the bronze, yellow, and scarlet autumn leaves, carefully plucking at berries, buds and other edibles. Seeing as many as thirty ptarmigan on Gros Morne during one quick visit is not difficult, but many of the birds of autumn do not survive winter, and it is difficult to find a handful that will nest in spring.

Ruffed Grouse and Spruce Grouse—both introduced from the mainland as game birds, and now occasionally seen in lowland forest in Gros Morne. **American Pipit and Horned Lark**—these species nest in the exposed rocky barrens of the Long Range highlands, and are often seen on Gros Morne mountain.

Horned lark.

American pipit.

© Michael Burzynski

Covey of rock ptarmigan on Gros Morne mountain.

View from Old Crow, near Gros Morne.

FROM TUCKAMORE TO TUNDRA

WHEN NEWFOUNDLAND GRADUATED FROM *TERRA incognita* to *Terra Nova* some 500 years ago, a series of changes began in the Island's plant and animal life. The most visibly affected ecosystem is the forest. Even the "pine clad hills" of the old Newfoundland national anthem are barely a memory in most parts of the Island.

ELFIN FOREST OF THE SEACOAST

On approaching the coast, the first indication of marine influence is the condition of the forest: trees get steadily smaller, more contorted, and more densely intertwined. The forest is pruned by onshore gusts that hurl salt spray far inland. Prevailing winds blast vegetation with ice crystals in winter and with grit in summer. Exposed needles and buds dry up and die, weak branches break off, and slowly the wind sculpts growing coastal trees into a stooped, streamlined forest that flows and swells inland like a brushy green wave.

NOTEPAD

Tuckamore or *Tuck* is the Newfoundland term for the dwarfed and twisted white spruce and balsam fir trees of this forest. According to the *Dictionary of Newfoundland English*, it is a combination of two words: *tucking*, meaning tugging or pulling (as in "tucking a net"), and *more*, an obsolete term for root. This is a perfect description of this weird vegetation of exposed roots and twisted trunks that shred clothing, grapple with legs, and rip the laces out of boots. The tenacity, ubiquity, and sculptural aesthetics of tuckamore led to its adoption as a symbol for Gros Morne National Park.

© Michael Burzynski

Tuckamore tunnel.

Coastal tuckamore... grows in tangled thickets...

that stretch along the coast for kilometres.

Tuckamore grows all along the exposed coastline of the park, around lakes, and on the wind-blasted flanks and summits of hills. Newfoundland's tuckamore is equivalent to the *krummholz* of the Alps. It is as difficult to push through as the wiry salal of the British Columbia coast and a lot more painful, because the prickly green crowns of tuckamore conceal an understory of sharp skeletal branches that can rip through trousers and skin.

At the upper shore, just beyond the reach of the waves, tuckamore starts as a tight ground-hugging mat of interwoven branches—barely deep enough to shade the crowberry or hide the tiny gentians and primroses that flower there in summer. Inland from this moss-like ground cover, the "canopy" of the elfin forest sweeps upward in a wind-shaped curve. The springy upper branches are so densely intertwined that clergyman U. Z. Rule wrote that in the 1860s "[walking] alongshore between Bonne Bay and Cow Head, I sometimes used the sloping surface of tuckamore as a couch to rest upon." This activity is not unheard of today. And explorer W. E. Cormack wrote in 1822: "The spruce-fir thickets are often only a few inches in height, the trees hooked and entangled together in such a manner as to render it practicable to walk upon, but impossible to walk through them." This is a forest for gnomes or elves—a scene right out of J. R. R. Tolkien's Middle Earth.

Tuckamore grows all along the exposed coast, but there are four exceptional places in the park to see it: the trails around Lobster Cove Head, the Old Mail Road Trail between Bakers Brook and Green Point, Green Point Campground, and Steve's Trail at Broom Point.

LOWLAND FOREST

Almost all of the forest in Gros Morne National Park grows on the lowlands. This is also where all the people live, so this forest has been cut for several generations to build and heat homes; to fashion schooners, dories, skiffs, and flats; and to construct lobster traps, floats, and other fishing gear. One of the agreements made by the park with local communities was to allow wood cutting for domestic use for two generations in parts of the lowland forest.

Hillside of birch in autumn colours.

Many tree and understory species typical of the Acadian Forest Region that covers the nearby Maritimes do not occur in the forests of the Island of Newfoundland. Typical trees of the park's boreal forest are black spruce, white spruce, balsam fir, eastern larch, white birch, mountain maple, speckled alder, green alder, and mountain ash, with small quantities of trembling aspen, balsam poplar, white pine, and red maple, as well as scattered pin cherry, choke cherry, black ash, and yellow birch. Bonne Bay is effectively the northern limit in Newfoundland for

Fir and spruce cloak the Southeast Hills.

Indian pipe, a flowering saprophyte.

Bunchberry, or *crackerberry*.

Twinflower, a fragrant forest groundcover.

yellow birch, red maple, white pine, black ash, pin cherry, and trembling aspen. This enriched boreal forest grows in the Lomond area of the park, and extends southwards along the coast past Corner Brook.

Balsam fir is a much more important tree in the forest of the west coast than it is elsewhere in Newfoundland. This seems to be because of the low frequency of wildfires. Where there were cutovers in the past, an almost solid fir forest has grown up. Here and there are grey patches where balsam fir stands have been killed by high populations of hemlock looper caterpillars. They not only eat young needles, but eventually chew their way into the older leaves as well—completely defoliating trees in a summer. The patchiness of the forest is easily seen from Wigwam Pond lookoff.

Recently killed trees look brown from a distance. Older grey stands of trees killed by hemlock looper in the 1980s are seen along Bakers Brook Falls, Berry Hill Pond, and Stuckless Pond trails. The trunks are festooned with brown and yellow-green old man's beard lichen. Carpenter ants and beetle larvae riddle the fungus-softened wood. Wind-thrown trees lie at all angles, slowly rotting back into soil. Raspberry bushes form a solid green understory, and white birch and balsam fir saplings reach for the sky. In wet openings, giant cow parsnips send up their pungent hairy leaves and stout bamboo-like flower stalks each year, often exceeding two metres in height. This grey forest of

Cow parsnip grows in rich soils everywhere in the park.

© Michael Burzynski

dead firs is actually a vibrant pocket of regrowth that is visited by moose, black bears, caribou, snowshoe hares, birds, and many species of insects, spiders, and other invertebrates. The nutrients locked up in the trees are recycled into the undisturbed soil, and support the growth of the new forest.

HIGHLAND FOREST

Although the mountains in Gros Morne would be considered mere hills in many places, climate makes their heights biologically alpine. In this park it is possible to start at sea level, climb up through boreal forest, cross the treeline, and continue into tundra and rock barrens—all in a few hours' walk. The treeline in the park lies at about 600 metres, only two-thirds of the way up the Long Range escarpment. Above that the trees are dwarfed, widely separated, and pruned tightly against the ground. On Gros Morne mountain itself, the treeline is even lower because growth is limited by the substrate of almost-pure silica and the cold air that pours off the surrounding hills. Above the treeline is a slice of the Arctic: patterned ground, tiny cushion plants, dwarf birches and willows, woodland caribou, Arctic hares, American pipits, horned larks, and rock ptarmigan.

Trees on this highland are stunted to the point of turning into a groundcover. Summer flowers such as harebells tower over spruce and larches that are scores of years old. On Big Hill a black spruce has grown five metres of trunk between its roots and crown, but none of that rises more than ankle high—it is a horizontal espalier. These trees creep across the ground from shelter to shelter in search of better growing conditions. Hollows offer some

Wind and cold dwarf spruce on the highlands.

wind protection, and capture insulating snow. Any branch that rises higher is nipped back in winter, pruning the trees into depression-filling hedges. Walking conditions on the highlands are sometimes treacherous because of this—any expanse of tightly woven branches on the ground could conceal a hole deep enough to hide a moose.

Any snow that falls on these highlands is either blasted away or wind packed into hard streamlined drifts—not fun for skiing, and worse for falling. Eroded edges of these dense drifts are patterned with layers that record their accumulation, mimicking the wood grain of the trees beneath them. Gusts raise a knee-high mist of ice crystals that races and eddies across the snow crust and rattles off drifts. White sky abuts seamlessly with the plateau at some vague horizon, and even though the light can be blinding, there are no shadows. Depth and distance come adrift in all this white, and vision starts to argue

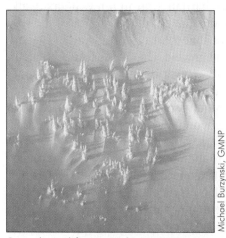

Snow-buried forest on the Long Range.

with balance. Only the occasional rock or stark twig pokes through to anchor perception to the white ground.

Taller treelets grow farther inland on the plateau, where they are spared by topography from the full force of the wind. This is the true highlands "tuck" that is encountered by summer hikers. Black spruce, white spruce, balsam fir, and the occasional white birch and green alder weave together into seemingly impenetrable green tangles. Most of these are not extensive, and hikers can walk around them. Others are large enough or positioned in such a way that it is necessary to pick a route through them. This is easily done by seasoned highland hikers, who walk along the periphery until they find a route that moose and caribou use. These "paths" can be a cross between an obstacle course and a

"Alpine" firs in a Long Range valley.

© Michael Burzynski

quagmire, but they are paths. Uninitiated hikers try to fight their way through the tuck—losing their skin, their patience, their tempers, and their way. The experience is akin to those bad dreams where it becomes harder and harder to move, and no amount of struggling and flailing and sweating and swearing will speed things up. Somehow Dante missed tuckamore in his descriptions of hell. Large patches of tuckamore can take hours to cross, and one Newfoundland forester (a Scot) has said, "You go in wearing trousers and come out wearing a kilt."

In places such as Big Level, tuckamore may never reproduce sexually. These trees probably arrived as seeds blown up from the forested slopes below. Where they found soil, the seedlings sprouted and grew. Short summers, a cool climate, and harsh winters have dwarfed the trees. Their lower branches root in the mossy soil, grow upward, and surround the original tree with clones of itself.

The real trees on the Long Range live in small valleys well inland from the edge of the escarpment. They grow as a patchy forest with clumps of spindly trees clustered tightly together. Between is open heathland or rock barrens. Most of the trees are black spruce and balsam fir. Fir does not

exhibit its typical conical growth form here. Branches at the base of the trees droop as though *weary* instead of sticking straight out from the trunk. The middle portions of the thin trunks are almost bare of branches, but the crowns wear a tight topknot of living twigs. These balsam fir look almost identical to the alpine fir of the Rockies, and are living in very similar conditions.

Farther inland, almost at the eastern boundary of the park, another forest begins. This is undisturbed Long Range forest, virgin woodland that has grown without human influence since trees returned to these highlands. Unfortunately, very little of this is included within the park. Stands just outside the park are now being rapidly clearcut for pulp, and within a decade or two this forest swill be gone.

© Michael Burzynski

Contorted forest, Berry Head Pond Trail.

THE GNOMES' FOREST

A different kind of forest develops along coastal roads, at the edges of lakes, and anywhere else that wind-blown snow smothers and crushes young conifers. Trunks wobble skyward in serpentine twists and contortions, their broken crowns grabbing arthriticly at the sky. Trunks split into twins, triplets, or entire copses of scrawny stems around a dead leader. What should be a forest of straight young trees is instead a confusion of bent knotted wood, limbs frozen in spasms that suggest yokes, hooks, snakes, cursive letters, avant-garde furniture, and elephant trunks. In a writhing of wood the twisted boles intertwine, disappearing one behind the other into their own gloom, enveloped in a mist of dripping lichen.

This contorted forest is shaped in winter. Then the snow blows off roads, lakes, and frozen ocean, and drifts deeply over these trees. The sheer weight of solid water bends their trunks to the snapping point. Trunks that fail during the winter are unable to bounce back up again when the snow melts—the wood fibres in their stems are torn and displaced. When trees lose their tops completely, lower branches take over and reach for light—eventually producing the multitrunked trees. When a tree's top is bent but not broken free, the tree will attempt to heal the damage and reach upward again—

resulting in a crooked trunk with a bulge and twist where the break has mended. Many trees endure multiple breaks and repairs, and the frozen convulsions of their trunks bear testimony to their struggle for survival. One of the best places to see this weird woodland is along Berry Head Pond Trail.

WAVE FOREST

There are hillsides in the park where the forest looks scruffier than usual, where trees grow in ragged green rows perpendicular to the slope, separated by grey blowdowns that are a shambles of dead and dying trunks, of fallen logs and saplings and upturned roots. These stands grow this way quite naturally, and the dead and living trees form a large-scale wave-like pattern.

Once again, wind is the force that moulds this forest. The waves of growth seem to be linked to strong prevailing winds that affect the tallest trees in the stand. One theory suggests that gusts blowing onto the face of the hill rock the tallest trees. This damages their roots and opens them to fungal infection. As these trees die, they expose those uphill to the wind. Needles fall, dead trunks collapse, light reaches the forest floor, and seedlings sprout. As the seedlings grow into saplings and eventually into mature trees, the progression of regenerating, dying, and dead forest moves like a slow wave up the hillside. Eventually the young trees are large enough to be affected by the wind, and start to weaken. Thus the process begins anew. The waves of live and dead trees look like a sloppy woodcutting operation, but can form where the hand of man has never set foot. At the mouths of Bakers Brook Pond and Western Brook Pond the wave forests face east—towards the winds that blow down off the Long Range. At Rocky Harbour it faces west—into winds off the sea.

Michael Burzynski, GMNP

Wave forest on hills near Rocky Harbour.

EXPLORING THE FOREST

Some trails that provide the best forest experience are Lookout, Lomond, Stanleyville, Stuckless Pond, Western Brook Pond, Bakers Brook Falls, and the lowland portion of the Gros Morne Mountain Trail. The lumbering history of the forest is interpreted with signs at the Wigwam Pond Lookoff and Lomond Day-use Area.

Sea stacks along the Green Gardens shore.

SPANTICKLES, SWILES, SCUMMIES, AND SCULLS

ALTHOUGH GROS MORNE'S COASTLINE IS MORE THAN 170 kilometres long (with another 60 kilometres within enclave communities), the park is essentially a terrestrial preserve. It extends only to the mean low water line, except in St. Pauls Inlet—the inner half of which is part of the park. Marine Biologist Bob Hooper has been exploring the waters off the park for more than 25 years and has made thousands of dives. He writes: "Every type of physical habitat in the Gulf of St. Lawrence Marine Region occurs along the Gros Morne coast. The marine plants and invertebrates of this area are especially notable because of the high diversity of Arctic and temperate species, some of which are extremely rare in Newfoundland. In fact, almost all of the marine plant and animal species found along the shores of eastern Canada can be seen in Bonne Bay."

BONNE BAY

Bonne Bay has had different names through time. In the mid-1500s the Basques whaled along the park coastline and named the major bay Baya *Ederra*, meaning "beautiful bay." The French later changed this to *Belle Baie*, and *Bonne Baie*, and from there it was only a tiny step to the anglicized version Bonne Bay (rhymes with Bombay). Bonne Bay is actually two connected fjords and the East Arm is by far the deeper of the two.

Like some Asian deities, Bonne Bay has more than the usual complement of arms. Worse yet, the arms of the bay have different local and official names: To the northeast is East Arm (locally called Main Arm) and to the southwest is South Arm (locally called Western Arm). The East Arm has two extensions: one to the north called Eastern Arm (or Deer Arm), and one to the southeast called, remarkably, Southeast Arm. East Arm and South Arm wrap around The Neck (the Lomond peninsula), and join at The Tickle to flow out of the mouth of the bay (between Eastern Head to the south, and Salmon Point to the north). And that is not the end of it: the East Arm has an extremely cold bottom, but in local terminology *the bottom of the bay* is its back (or its head, or its tail).

There is a remarkable diversity of organisms in East Arm, with disjunct arctic species in the cold depths, and warmer-water species near the surface. Gadds Harbour, opposite Norris Point, is particularly rich in different kinds of seaweeds. In fact, except for a handful of species, all of the seaweeds found around the Island's 6,000 kilometre shoreline grow there. Because of the diversity and richness of the bay, Memorial University of Newfoundland has operated a marine biology research laboratory in Norris Point since 1970.

Bonne Bay at sunset.

Michael Burzynski, GMNP

East Arm's waters are layered, or stratified into different temperatures and salinities, and this accounts for the great diversity of life found there. In the same way that isolated arctic plants and animals survive on islands of tundra atop the highlands of the Long Range, some arctic plants and animals also survive in the depths of the arm. These organisms probably reached East Arm after the last glaciation when arctic conditions would have prevailed here. As the ice melted back and the whole coast warmed up, these organisms survived in the depths of East Arm and were not completely replaced by warmer-water plants and animals. Now they are isolated from others of their species by hundreds of kilometres of warm water.

East Arm is a natural refrigerator. Its bottom is constantly maintained at -1°C. The shape of this bay and the physical properties of water cause the refrigeration. East Arm is extremely deep (reaching 230 metres), but the entrance to East Arm, at The Tickle, is only about 15 metres deep. This isolates the bay from the Gulf of St. Lawrence, and allows layering (stratification) to occur. Layering is possible because the colder and saltier that water gets, the denser it is. Denser water sinks, and warmer, less-salty water rises. Water in the East Arm of Bonne Bay becomes separated into layers of different densities, based on the layers' temperatures and salinities. Gulf of St. Lawrence water that flows in with the rising tide does not mix below the East Arm's uppermost layer.

As surface waters of East Arm warm, an obvious thermocline/ halocline (a boundary based on differences in temperature and salinity), develops within a metre of the surface. Often the boundary between the two layers is knife sharp. From above, the boundary distorts the view of the bottom as ripples in its surface act like a warped lens. After a heavy rainfall, river water brown with soil acids stains the upper layer of the bay, and the difference between layers above and below the thermocline is even more obvious. Seen through a diving mask there is warm brown brackish water at the surface, and cold, saltier, crystal-clear water below, with a rippling silver boundary between. This is only the top layer in this stratified bay, and its temperature can reach 20°C.

Salt lowers the freezing temperature of water, so seawater does not freeze at 0°C, but remains liquid to -1.6°C. Salt is forced out of water as it freezes, so sea ice is effectively lumps of fresh water with unfrozen brine in between. Cold water also holds more dissolved oxygen than warm water.

In January, ice starts to form as the bay cools. Ice is not as dense as water, and floats at the surface. Dense supercooled brine seeps out of the freezing seawater, and sinks into the depths of the bay, chilling the bottom waters, increasing their salinity, and bringing down oxygen from the surface. In this way the icy waters at the bottom of the East Arm are always maintained at -1°C, and are

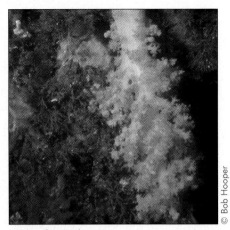

© Bob Hooper

Red soft-coral.

J.D. Clarke, GMNP

Lobster on guard.

J. D. Clarke, GMNP

Green sea-urchins and sea anemones.

Lion's-mane jellyfish.

Waved whelk, a predatory snail.

the thermal equivalent of the Arctic Ocean.

Tidal rapids at The Tickle in Bonne Bay and beneath the St. Pauls bridge have the densest and most diverse marine life in the park area. Tidal water flowing into and out of the bays each day carries small plants and animals and suspended nutrients. Filter-feeding animals flourish in the rapids, since there is lots of food suspended in the incoming and outgoing waters. Currents through the rapids also reduce predators and slow ice formation. Seabirds, seals, and other animals can live there when all other seawater is ice covered. These tidal rapids are considered to be the most spectacular marine assets in the park area.

Because of its colourful marine life and clear waters, the East Arm of Bonne Bay is well known among scuba divers. However, it also has strong currents, steep drop offs, and unpredictable winds that can whip up rough water. One well-known dive is below towering Shag Cliff (opposite Norris Point), where the water is clear, cold, and extremely deep. The cliff continues sheer underwater, plunging into darkness far below. Attached to the rocks are clusters of small white shells called brachiopods, or lamp shells. They cling to limestone that contains the fossils of ancestors that lived in a warm Ordovician sea. Brachiopods are the Luddites of the animal world. They shun new-fangled fads such as eyes, fins, lungs, opposable thumbs, and digital watches, and have lived almost unchanged for half a billion years.

Cunners are common shoreline scavengers.

ROCKY SHORE INTERTIDAL ZONE

Safer and easier than diving, and far more accessible, is a visit to the intertidal zone. For half of the day the intertidal zone is part of the sea, but for the other half its seaweed-thatched rocks are abandoned by the retreating water, and left to drip dry. Miniature seas lie trapped in rocky hollows on the shore at low tide. These tidepools are windows into the ocean, moist fragments of sea left behind twice each day by the falling water. The best time to visit the intertidal zone is on the falling tide.

Water in the uppermost pools is refreshed only on the highest tides, and they are often stagnant, clogged with mats of green algae, decomposing kelp stems, and shell fragments. Their high temperatures and acidity render them devoid of larger animals—a microbial broth.

Encrusting the most exposed rocks are barnacles, their shells resembling miniature white volcanoes. Barnacles are planktonic when young, floating from place to place with the currents. They soon settle down on rocks and other surfaces, gluing themselves in place head down and building up white shell walls. As they grow older, their limestone walls get larger and algae stain them yellow. Barnacles live out their lives within these individual fortresses, exposing their feet whenever water covers them. Waving their feet through the water like nets they snag particles of food and pull them inside the shell to be consumed. The only other part of a barnacle that gets exposed solves another problem. These barnacles are hermaphrodites—they have both male and female sexual organs. They cannot move around and meet each other, yet find it more efficient to mate with several different partners. To accomplish this, each has a very long penis that does the wandering for them, probing around the colony until it meets a receptive partner.

Michael Burzynski, GMNP

Intertidal platform and tide pools at Green Gardens.

Dog whelks and barnacles.

Purple sea-stars.

© Michael Burzynski

Red-gilled nudibranch.

Bob Hooper, GMNP

Blue mussels feeding.

© Michael Burzynski

Rockweed in a cloud of mysid shrimp.

© Michael Burzynski

Hermit crab living in a waved whelk shell.

GMNP

Farther down, rubbery brown knotwrack and bladderwrack cling to rocks in the intertidal zone. At low tide these seaweeds drape the rock, but at high tide gas bladders along their stems raise them upright to take advantage of the light. Wind-driven ice pans mow them off in spring. This leaves boulders with bare tops and shorn sides, but with lush seaweed growth at the base and in cracks where the ice could not reach.

Packed around seaweed holdfasts and crowded in cracks and depressions are clusters of blue mussels, their shells partly agape showing the intake and waste siphons that they use to gather microscopic food. Periwinkles graze on the thin film of algae that cover rock surfaces, and an occasional predatory dogwhelk slides along the rock in search of its next meal—perhaps a mussel, or a barnacle. Rock crabs tiptoe across the bottom in search of live and dead prey. Empty crab exoskeletons lie limply among the rocks where old tight shells have been molted, exposing new, better-fitting armour underneath. Hermit crabs scuttle about in their snail-shell homes and grapple with each other for food and more commodious accommodations. Tortoiseshell limpets graze across rock surfaces like animated suction cups—leaving faint meandering trails where they have scraped away the thin layer of algae. Sideswimmers and other small shrimp-like animals scoot through the water, constantly looking for food and safe hiding places.

Some tidepools are steep-sided potholes that are eroded when pebbles are churned around by wave action. Others are the result of chemical and ice weathering, as seen on the tidal platforms at Lobster Cove Head and Green Gardens. A few, however, are excavated in limestone by marine life. They start as small depressions that catch water during high tide. Algae colonize these mini tidepools, and acids released by them and their decomposition soften the rock. The pools enlarge, and soon periwinkles enter and feed by rasping algae off

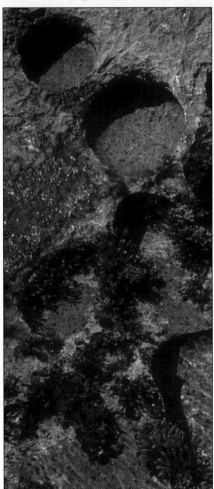

© Michael Burzynski

Solution potholes in Cow Head limestone.

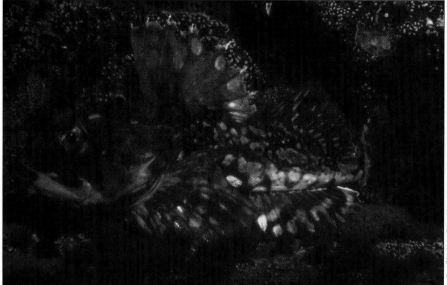

Shorthorn sculpin.

the rock—speeding up the erosion. As the pools grow, small arches form where adjacent pools join. This is truly erosion at a snail's pace.

Large pools closest to the sea edge often have fish in them. Flatfish, rock gunnels, sticklebacks, and tadpole-shaped snailfish, and even juvenile lumpfish are sometimes trapped there between the tides. One of the most beautiful fish of these pools is the shorthorn sculpin. Hated by fishermen as a bait eater, and reviled by children who fish from wharves, sculpins are called *scummies* in Newfoundland. They are bottom fish with a laid-back lifestyle. They match the bottom in tone, and their intricate pattern of spots and blotches and their fringed fins help them look like rock or seaweed. They have wide mouths with thick lips, and huge golden eyes. They lie in wait for food to pass by, or swim lazily after it. Their heads and gill covers are decorated with spines, and when disturbed sculpins bloat themselves with water or air, erecting fins and spines to appear large and dangerous. But sculpins are the butterflies of the seashore. They are harmless and easy to approach, and fan their wide fins out as they swim slowly away.

Green sea-urchins huddle in spiny clusters in the deepest pools, decorating themselves with shells, seaweed scraps, and small rocks as camouflage from gulls. Any urchin so unlucky as to be seen is quickly hoisted aloft and smashed on the rocks, or carried to shore, flipped on its back, and pecked open from underneath (actually through its mouth). An urchin moves about slowly on hundreds of sucker-tipped tube feet that protrude between the ranks of spines. Like some marine Medusa, the entire animal is surrounded by writhing serpentine "feet," and it somehow coordinates these feet and its myriad defensive spines without a brain. With these hydraulic limbs it can slowly right itself when flipped upside down. The sun-bleached shells of dead urchins are decorated with an intricate pattern of minute holes and tiny bumps that mark where tube feet and spines were attached.

Sea-anemones wave fleshy tentacles from the tops of their stubby bodies. Cells on the tentacles are equipped with poisoned darts, and can stun and hold small animals that swim too close. Crowds of varicoloured purple seastars live in tangles of purple, orange, brown, and pink at the outer edge of the shore. They are predators that kill and digest mussels and other prey in a multiarmed embrace. In the deepest pools and offshore, long blades of leathery brown kelp wave in the water. Colander wrack is a darker kelp, with a blade perforated by hundreds of holes like the aftermath of a shotgun attack. Dulse, one of the edible seaweeds, shines like red stained glass when held up against the sun, while sea lettuce is bright green.

Dark cunners (*conners*) swarm along the edge of the shore in loose schools. Small toothy reddish predators, they are second only to sculpins as the least appreciated fish of the coast. They hibernate under rocks on the seafloor through cold weather. In deeper water, parts of the seafloor are dominated by pink calcareous algae. These seaweeds produce coral-like crusts and balls as their filaments are encrusted with calcium carbonate from the water. The crusts are made up of small branching growths that completely cover rocks, bottles, shells, and anything else that stays still long enough. Cavities in the pink crusts are used by many small animals as shelters. Fishermen call these coralline lumps *live rock* or *red rock*. Sunbleached knobby masses of these algae often wash up on shore and are usually mistaken for coral. The only true hard corals in this area are small deep-water species.

The most accessible tidepools are at Lobster Cove Head, Broom Point, Cow Head, and Green Point. Spectacular pools also cover the intertidal platform at Green Gardens. There is enough life in and around the intertidal zone to keep naturalists occupied until the returning tide nudges them off the beach.

TIDES AND THE COAST

The moon and tides affect plants, animals, and us. They play an important role in the timing of natural phenomena such as the egg laying frenzy of capelin along beaches, and the upriver runs of trout and Atlantic Salmon. Egg and sperm release by marine animals and even some brown seaweeds is timed by the phases of the moon.

In English and many other languages, the words *month* and *Monday* are derived from the name of our celestial partner, the moon. *Month* refers to the 28 days that it takes for the moon to complete an orbit around the earth. Since the moon orbits in the same direction that the earth rotates on its axis, it takes 24 hours and 50 minutes for a point on the earth's surface to reappear directly beneath the moon—one *lunar day*. During each lunar day there are two complete tidal cycles, with the tides alternating from high to low to high to low with about six-and-a-quarter hours between each phase. The actual times and heights of tides vary from day to day. Tides in restricted bays such as East Arm and St. Pauls Inlet have a lower range and are slightly later than elsewhere along the coast.

During the summer it is easy to estimate the time of high and low tides (within an hour or so). High range *spring tides* occur when the moon is full or new, with high water around noon and midnight, and low water around six in the morning and evening. Each successive day, the morning and afternoon tides will be about 50 minutes later than the day before, until the month's quarter moons are reached. Then the tides will be low range *neap tides*: low around noon and midnight and high around six in the morning and evening.

The word spring is derived from the Old English word *springan*, meaning "a welling," and has nothing to do with the season. Spring tides usually have the greatest high-low range of the month—they rise highest and fall farthest—although storm winds can also influence the height of tides. *Neap* means something akin to "nipped," and refers to the lowest ranging tides of the month. The greatest tidal range along the park coast is about two metres.

COBBLE BEACHES

One of the most interesting parts of any beach is the wave-lodged flotsam and jetsam of the wrack line. Black tumbles of seaweed surround driftwood, old lobster traps, abandoned nets, rope and buoys, feathers, shells, and fragments of old boats. The wrack line is a place of juxtaposition: of treasure with garbage, of live with dead, of land with sea. Because of the nutrient value of the cast-up vegetation and animal fragments, some crustaceans, flies, and other small animals depend entirely on the wrack.

The largest driftwood is usually the sun-bleached and decaying reminder of great storms, heaved well above the usual tides. Lower down, there are often several thin lines of black wrack drying in the sun. They indicate different tide heights in the fortnightly cycle, where the sea has deposited wave-shorn seaweed (locally called *killup* or *kelp*) on successively lower high tides. These lines will be erased in the following days as the tide moves back to its high range. Summer storms throw up knots of cable-like kelps, heaps of eelgrass, and brown rockweed. October storms leave large quantities of *red moss*. In places, the seaweed piles up as metre-deep drifts tens of metres long. These seaweeds are harvested locally as a natural fertilizer for the peaty soil of roadside gardens.

Storm-driven waves heave large cobbles ashore along the most exposed beaches, and high berms build up. They rise three to four metres above sea level, and contain head-sized rocks—a good indication of the power of storm waves. Even during quiet seas, these shores rumble and grind as waves roll rock against rock. The sea winnows and sorts the rock rubble,

Lobster boat going down a slipway at Sally's Cove.

leaving only cobbles and boulders that the waves are incapable of carrying away. This is why all of the rocks on a stretch of beach are usually of similar size and weight.

There is little visible plant or animal life along cobble shores, since the rock is continually being shifted by waves. Even boats and the carcasses of beached whales break up quickly on these shores (usually within a summer), and porous, oily whale bones are ground into fragments by the mill of rolling boulders.

On most cobble beaches in the park, the common rocks are quartzite and Long Range granite and gneiss. Gneiss is the oldest rock, and some of the most resistant to erosion. Its colours and patterns of stripes, and the texture

Lobster traps driven ashore by a storm.

and sheen of the polished cobbles brighten any walk on the beach. Here you can see features in the rock that are obscured by lichens and weathering on the highlands. The steep slope of the berms and the smoothly rounded cobbles make walking difficult. The shore north of Sally's Cove is one of the best places to see large berms.

SANDY SHORES

Gros Morne has two large sand beaches on salt water. One lies at the mouth of Western Brook and the other curls in a crescent around Shallow Bay. These blond sands are another legacy of glaciation—they are ground up and sifted remnants of Long Range rock. The melting ice left a veneer of rock rubble over the land. At higher sea levels, waves washed and sorted these moraines and tills, and rivers carried sand to sea. Currents drift the sand into bays, and waves drive it ashore. Onshore winds pick up grains from the beach, and bounce and tumble them inland. Grains cluster into ripples, ripples grow into dunes, and dunes migrate inland.

Grass is a crucial landscaping agent here. Not the citified greenery of golf courses and suburban lawns, but a tough and tenacious plant called marram grass. Marram grows about knee high, with tall wheat-like seedheads. It colonizes moving sand, sending fibrous roots deep into a dune to tap its moist interior. As they spread, the roots of marram grass stitch the loose dune sand together. Dunes at Western Brook reach 18 metres high, and eroded sand faces reveal layers of black soil, sometimes five or six in a stack, that mark stages in the growth, stabilization, and vegetation of the dunes. Dunes are a transient feature of the landscape—storms can destroy them, and rising sea level will eventually erase them. Marram grass can withstand the baking sun, winter's ice, drought, moving sand, and salt spray, but it cannot withstand trampling. Please stay on marked trails and boardwalk dune crossings when exploring park beaches.

Sand beaches are quiet places. Because of the gentle slope of the beach and the protection of coves, waves are restrained. Wind hisses through the marram, tracing delicate circles in the sand with spiky leaf tips, exhuming silvery skeletons of a forest buried as the dunes moved inland, then reburying it grain by grain. Strings of fox and moose tracks dimple the dunes, recording a lazy morning walk to the beach. Fibrous clumps of marram grass roots dry where the sand has fallen away. In the warmth of the day, sand cascades down dune faces in small fans. Like untamed hourglasses, these trickles mark the passage of the day and symbolize both the creation and destruction of dunes.

Offshore are eelgrass beds and rocks covered with Irish moss, and burrowing animals such as softshell clams, sand dollars, razor clams, and many species of marine worms. Amethystine Arctic-red jellyfish pulse through the sun-warmed shallows trailing threadbare trains of red tentacles. Many end up

Warm sandy shallows near Lower Head.

Water and wind rearrange the sand each year.

Marram grass stabilizes dunes.

as lens-shaped wrecks on the beach. Shorn of their red tentacles and glistening purple on the sand, they remain beautiful in death.

Flounders lie on the soft bottom, mimicking patches of sand. When touched they rocket off, undulating across the bottom at high speed to stir up mud. They then double back and hide in the clouds that they have thrown up. Silvery schools of sardine-sized fish flash through the water like raindrops in a sunshower. Below, coils of mud mark the entrances to worm holes in the seafloor, and dense underwater meadows of dark green eelgrass sway in time with the waves. Moon snails plough through the mud in search of clams and other prey, their grey watery bodies supporting smooth round shells.

Small flocks of black-legged sanderlings scurry along the edge of the waves, running out with the dropping water, then retreating landward with the incoming lap. They peck at small animals tossed up or exposed by the

Kelp and other seaweeds wash up after storms.

sea, and move with a clockwork frenzy.

In June, at spring tide, capelin *sculls* (schools) hover off coarse sand beaches. When the water is at its highest the fish dart for the shore, and all along the beach they tumble out of waves and onto the sand. They writhe out of water, males with females, eggs and sperm mingling in the wet sand. The next wave dislodges the fish, and the process is repeated farther along the beach. Some capelin exhaust themselves, or are hurled too high on the beach, dying as the mating frenzy continues around them. As the tide falls the line of mating fish thins and then disappears and the scull moves offshore.

A silvery wrack line of small dead fish dries in the sun. It is picked over by gulls that have gorged themselves to a state of aerodynamic instability. Flounders, pout, and other fish move into the shallows and feast on whatever eggs they can reach, bloating themselves almost into immobility. The sand at the upper tide line is thick with eggs, each glued to sand and to other eggs. There the eggs mature for two weeks until the next high spring tide, when hatchling fish wash back into the sea.

ESTUARIES

Because there are few large rivers in the park area, there are not many extensive estuaries—places where fresh water and salt water mix. St. Pauls Inlet is considered estuarine because the flow of freshwater off the land and restricted mixing in the Inlet reduce the salinity of the entire bay. Eastern Arm and the mouth of the Lomond River (East Arm Barachois) both have well developed estuaries.

These estuaries are tidal, and low water exposes mud flats and tangles of bright green algae called sausageweed or intestineweed. Marine clams and worms live in the mud, and schools of sticklebacks (often called *spantickles* and *pinfish* in Newfoundland) and other small fish dart through beds of eelgrass. Red-breasted mergansers with strings of chicks in tow are often seen at Eastern Arm and Lomond, and greater yellowlegs and sandpipers wade along shore probing the mud for small prey.

Ospreys hover over estuaries and river mouths while searching for fish, then dive into the water, and struggle back into the air dripping and juggling a fish in their talons. They are big birds, but often they barely clear the tops of trees as they flap back to the nest with lunch for the kids. Bald eagles nest in old pines and on cliffs, building huge twiggy aeries. The white heads and tails of the adults are visible even at great distances, but the brown young are well camouflaged, and it is usually their calls for food that reveal them. Eagles fish in the shallows, scavenge along the shores and on land, and occasionally rob flying gulls and ospreys of food.

Estuary and salt marsh at Glenburnie.

Oysterleaf.

Sea rocket – a pungent mustard.

Beach pea.

Seaside plantain.

Dwarf coastal iris.

Seabeach groundsel.

Seabeach sandwort.

Roseroot.

SALTMARSHES

A saltmarsh usually develops around an estuary where grassy vegetation traps and stabilizes shoreline mud. In the park, as in the rest of Newfoundland, saltmarshes are uncommon and small. The largest and most beautiful saltmarsh in the park area is at St. Pauls—one of the most unusual and fascinating habitats in the park area.

The *Green* on the south side of the mouth of St. Pauls Bay was long used as a pasture, and large areas are fenced. A winding, rutted, dirt road connects the fishing premises at the tip to the main road. This area is part of the community of St. Pauls. The grassy flats are flooded with salt water only during very high tides. The grasses on the cobble and sand flats are punctuated with clumps of blue-flowered dwarf coastal-iris, yellowish moonwort ferns, deep-blue island gentians, pale-blue marsh felwort, spurred gentian, and wild strawberry. Silverweed runners crisscross the sand with a scarlet net, and buttercup-yellow flowers shine brightly amid rosettes of glossy leaves that flash silvery undersides in the wind.

The lowest parts of the marsh are a muddy expanse of sedges and rushes surrounding warm brackish pools filled with green-brown algae. Footprints puncture the mud, and succulent-stemmed glasswort (or *samphire*) plants fill the holes. Emerald green in summer, they turn ruby red in autumn.

These marshes and estuaries attract shorebirds on their southward migration—starting in early July. First come flocks of adult birds, followed several weeks later by their young of the year. Most nest around James Bay and the Arctic, and have already flown a long way to get here. They are hungry, and must fatten up in order to have enough energy to sustain them on the rest of their flight to southern wintering ground. They feed singly or in small flocks on small crustaceans, worms, and soft-bodied animals buried in the mud.

Michael Burzynski, GMNP

Marsh in St. Pauls Inlet.

Alpine bistort.

Silverweed flowers and runners.

Spurred gentian.

Island gentian.

Most common among the shorebirds are semipalmated sandpipers, white-rumped sandpipers, semipalmated plovers, black-bellied plovers, and greater yellowlegs. Mixed in are smaller numbers of golden plovers, whimbrels, hudsonian godwits and ruddy turnstones. The shorebirds are followed by hunting peregrine falcons and occasional gyrfalcons in autumn.

LIFE OFFSHORE

Farther offshore are the large marine animals. Seals (sometimes called *swiles*) bob in the swells, watching those who explore the wet edge of the sea. Sharks are relatively frequent visitors to these waters, and get tangled in nets every few years. Most common are blue sharks and porbeagles about two metres long, but far larger basking sharks are sometimes seen—some fully eight metres from nose to tail—harmless animals that glide through the surface waters with their toothless mouths agape, filtering out plankton. Atlantic sturgeon, ocean sunfish, giant bluefin tuna, and swordfish have also been caught here on occasion. About 200 tuna and many pilot whales were harpooned in Bonne Bay in the 1920s for fox feed.

The three most commonly seen whales are minke, humpback, and pilot. The best whale watching in the park is at Lobster Cove Head Lighthouse, the shorefront of Woody Point, the wharf at Norris Point, and Trout River Harbour. Watch in spring and autumn when sand lance, Atlantic herring, squid, or mackerel are schooling, preferably on a windless day when there are low swells. Listen for puffs and snorts of breath, and search for long black shapes breaking the water. Ask locally whether whales have been seen recently, and check at the park Visitor Centre and the Lobster Cove Head Lighthouse where daily sightings are recorded.

Atlantic Walruses—once lived along park beaches. A tusk was found at Trout River in 12,000-year-old sediments, and a 710 year-old skull washed up at Cow Head in 1993. The name Cow Head is probably derived from a French name for walrus—*vache de mer*, or "sea cow." Visiting English naturalist Henry Reeks wrote in 1871: "From the quantity of 'tusks' picked up…the walrus must have been an inhabitant of the island…. The tusks are frequently used as 'row-locks' by the settlers: I saw many that had evidently been used in this way for many years." There are no records of live walruses in park waters during the last two centuries—they were probably extirpated here by those hunting for oil and ivory.

Harbour Seals—usually seen in St. Pauls Inlet in summer. Some are residents of the Inlet, and there are probably fifty or sixty along the entire park coast. They often haul out onto rocks in the Inlet to bask at low tide. The boat tour is an excellent way to see them.

Harp Seals—swim by the park in the hundreds of thousands each spring and autumn. In spring they whelp at the edge of the sea ice. Seals are still

Harbour seals, St. Pauls Inlet.

Sheldon Stone, GMNP

© Michael Burzynski

Humpback whale.

hunted offshore for meat and pelts, as they have been since humans first lived along this coast.

Grey Seals—relatively common between Trout River and Bonne Bay in late summer.

Hooded Seals and Ringed Seals—both winter along the park coast in small numbers.

Pilot Whales—(*potheads* or *blackfish*) toothed whales that travel in pods of a dozen or more and feed on fish and squid, usually in park waters in the autumn. They grow to about 6 metres long. Their large, hooked dorsal fin is sometimes mistaken for a shark's.

Minke Whales—small solitary baleen whales that live in the park area from thaw to freeze. Although frequently seen feeding near shore, there may only be a few in the area at a time. Maximum length is about 8.5 metres. About the only signs of a minke whale feeding offshore are its loud exhalations and the low profile of back and hooked dorsal fin. Sometimes, however, they lunge feed through a school of fish at the surface, displaying white baleen and a white-banded flipper. Minke and pilot whales were hunted in Newfoundland waters until 1972, when the last North American whale fishery ceased.

Humpback Whales—baleen whales that often feed on capelin in park waters in the spring. They are easily identified by a stumpy dorsal fin and the sharp hunch in their back as they dive. Their spouts are loud and obvious, and they often display their tails at the start of deep dives. These whales sometimes show up again in the autumn when schools of mackerel and herring are moving along the shore.

Finback Whales and Blue Whales—both are baleen whales, and can reach lengths of 24 metres and 27 metres respectively. The latter is the largest animal in the world. Both are rare in park waters.

Atlantic Bowhead Whales and North Atlantic Right Whales—large baleen whales that were extirpated from these waters by whaling.

Sperm Whales—largest of the toothed whales, reaching up to 18 metres. Two carcasses have washed ashore on this coast in the last 20 years.

Atlantic Killer Whales (*Orcas*)—toothed whales that can reach lengths of 10 metres, hunt in small packs, and feed on seals, porpoises, large fish, and other whales. Sightings are extremely uncommon in the park area. A stone effigy found at the 4,500 year old Port au Choix Maritime Archaic Indian cemetery clearly represents the body and tall dorsal fin of a killer whale.

Belugas (*White Whales*)—grow about four metres long, and are pure white, with no dorsal fin. Belugas are toothed whales, and one wanders into park waters about every decade, either from the Arctic or from the St. Lawrence estuary.

White-sided Dolphins—relatively common, especially in autumn. They reach a length of almost three metres, and often swim in large pods. When herring or mackerel are schooling, there can be from 100 to 500 dolphins in Bonne Bay. They are often very acrobatic jumpers.

Harbour Porpoises—the smallest members of the whale family in our area, reaching only 1.5 metres. It has small peg-like teeth, and does not jump clear of the water. Because of its loud breathing, it is known as a *puffing pig*. The name "porpoise" is derived from the Latin words *porcus* and *piscis* meaning "pig fish."

THE ICE PAN COMETH

Ice can be both a protective and a destructive force in the lives of marine organisms. In early winter, as cold air gradually lowers the surface temperature of the Gulf to -2°C (the freezing point of seawater), shard-like crystals of freshwater ice form. They are separated from each other by a brine of salty water forced out of the ice during the freezing process. Called *brash* or *slush* ice, this slurry dampens wave movement, and as the slurry shifts around on the water surface the crystals clump into soft rounded pancake ice. Severe storms usually initiate ice formation, and as the

Porbeagle shark that got tangled in a net.

water "catches over," sharp ice crystals can scour shoreline plants and animals off the rocks.

As winter progresses day by day, more ice crystals form and freeze together. Brine drains off along channels, and the ice pans become larger and more solid. An *ice foot* freezes to the shore, clinging solidly to the intertidal zone and growing thicker throughout the winter. It protects intertidal life from the bitter winter winds, and from ice scouring. When pack ice is blown against the shore it rides up and over the ice foot. The ice foot is usually the last sea ice to melt in spring, sometimes damming up freshwater runoff and causing the death of intertidal organisms.

THE FISHERY

The fishery for northern lobsters employs the largest number of fishermen in the park area, and has the highest dollar value. In the 1800s lobsters could be caught inshore by hand and were often used for bait. Now they are the focus of a tightly regulated fishery. The opening of the season is often delayed by ice offshore. Some years the harbours are still frozen, other years there are too many large ice pans on the water. Cold water also keeps the lobsters in a state of torpor, and they are uninterested in food. The biggest catches are usually early in the season.

Michael Burzynski, GMNP

Abandoned flat, St. Pauls Inlet.

The commercial fishery for Atlantic salmon ended around the Island of Newfoundland in 1992—the same year that the east coast Atlantic cod moratorium went into effect. The moratorium on Atlantic cod fishing began in 1993 in the park area. There is still a local fishery for Atlantic halibut, Newfoundland turbot, Canadian plaice, skate, flounders, Atlantic herring, Atlantic mackerel, capelin, lumpfish, snow crab, and toad crab. Other species that live offshore include spiny dogfish, squid, redfish, haddock, pollock, silver hake, giant scallops, blue mussels, horse mussels, shrimp, cunners, sculpin, Arctic cod, wolf-fish, eelpouts, and many others. Today many of these are reviled. Tomorrow they may be "underutilized species."

Cod migrate northward in early summer and southward in early winter, and these used to be the best times for fishing. Historically, many people from this coast followed the cod schools north to Labrador and then returned in the fall to sell their salted catch. This led to strong ties between families in the park area and the coastal communities in Labrador.

EXPLORING THE COAST

The best way to get a feel for the coast is from the water. Boat tours are offered from several communities, and small boats can also be chartered. For an even more intimate view of the water, sea kayak and sailboat tours are available on Bonne Bay. Coastal hiking is best on Lobster Cove Head, Green Gardens, Old Mail Road, and Western Brook Beach trails. The largest sandy beaches are at Shallow Bay and Western Brook Beach. A roadside exhibit at Gull Rocks interprets the marine life of East Arm.

View from Western Brook Pond Trail.

FLATOUT TO THE MOUNTAINS

GROS MORNE'S COASTAL LOWLANDS STRETCH FROM Rocky Harbour to the park's northern boundary. Beyond that the lowlands continue all the way up the Great Northern Peninsula. They comprise the flat wetlands and low ridges between the foot of the Long Range escarpment and the waters of the Gulf of St. Lawrence.

Lowland rock was buckled and faulted during the thrust and uplift of the Long Range. Subsequent erosion wore the rock down almost flat, and almost to sea level. The shale layers of the bedrock were eroded more deeply than the limestone strata, etching a large-scale pattern of ridges and hollows into the lowlands.

BOGS AND FENS

Forest grew on the well-drained limestone ridges, but these ridges impeded drainage of the lowlands. In moist hollows, accumulating organic matter from moisture-loving plants led to the growth of bogs and fens.

Bogs are wetlands dominated by the many species of sphagnum moss. Dead, partially decomposed sphagnum is the horticultural peat used by gardeners, and the live moss grows as moist mounds of red, green, yellow, or brown fleshy-looking, star-shaped plants. Individual plants can grow for many decades, and each year they add several millimetres to their height.

Coastal lowland, with the Long Range rising in the distance.

Peat dams separate flashets on a coastal lowland bog.

These mosses live in wet places, and have large, specialized, hollow cells in their "leaves" that act as containers for absorbing and holding water whenever it is available. Sphagnum is a good sponge and can hold many times its own weight in water. Once the moss starts to grow in a hollow, the hollow remains wet, no matter what the weather.

Sphagnum thrives on impoverished soils because it is able to extract and acquire nutrients that are unavailable to other plants. Like other mosses, it has no roots, and absorbs nutrients through its stems and leaves. To do this, sphagnum floods its surroundings with acid. The lowered pH breaks chemical bonds and mobilizes nutrients that the moss then quickly absorbs. Sphagnum is adapted to living in an acidic environment, but many plants are not, so the low pH created by the moss and by its decaying stems promotes the growth of more sphagnum while it deters competitors.

Like beavers and humans, sphagnum alters its surroundings to create a more favourable habitat. As it grows it spreads outwards, blanketing more ground. Each year's growth of moss covers up the dead stems and leaves of previous years, and wicks ground moisture up a bit higher. Decay is slowed almost to a stop by acidity, by the waterlogging that keeps out oxygen, and by the cool maintained by the blanket of dead plant matter. Below the living layer of moss in a bog is a mausoleum of moss ancestors, pickled into brown peat. They are preserved as they lived, with some compression by the accumulating layers above. Embalmed with the moss is anything that dropped onto the bog: seeds, wood, leaves, spores, pollen, dust, charcoal, insects, and occasionally larger animals and human artifacts. The peat becomes an archive of organic matter, a record of local growing conditions and vegetation.

Water does not percolate through a bog, and a thick layer of peat insulates the living plants at the surface from the mineral soil below. The only source of nutrients for the living plants at the bog surface is rain. The lowland bogs have been growing for about 9,000 years, and range between two and four metres deep. These bogs have filled the hollows between some of the limestone ridges, forming flat-topped plateau bogs. Like bread dough rising in a shallow pan, a growing sphagnum bog slowly raises the water table with it, spills into nearby forest, drowns the trees, and then grows in their stead.

There are many shallow ponds in the bogs. Most have rock bottoms that are a good indication of the depth of the nearby bogs. Peat does not accumulate in these lakes because the moving water carries oxygen right to the bottom, and bacterial and fungal decay is rapid. The dark brown water in the ponds is stained by organic acids from the nearby peat and forest. The rocks

Pitcherplant.

Great sundew.

Butterworts.

Horned bladderwort flowers.

and sand along the shores of these ponds are usually bleached white by the acids, and in some cases only resistant white quartz particles remain.

Yellow pondlilies bob on the dark surface of bog ponds, and trailing strands of insect-eating bladderworts lie in the shallows—green "feather boas" in the brown water. Pitcherplants cluster wide-mouthed in wait for prey along the shores, among glistening patches of wine-red sundews. Since these plants take "dietary supplements" in the form of insects and other prey, they too can make do with very meagre soil nutrients. The other plants that grow in bogs must either be extremely frugal, or extremely slow growing.

The most common bog plants on the park lowlands are heaths. These include bog laurel, leatherleaf, bog rosemary, and bog cranberry, with Labrador tea, sheep laurel, and rhodora on drier hummocks. Bakeapple is another typical bog plant, and perhaps the most valued berry in Newfoundland and Labrador. It looks like a large orange raspberry, and is only ripe when it is too soft to pick.

Fens are a different kind of wetland. Although they may have sphagnum mosses growing in them, the dominant plants are usually sedges and grasses. The peat produced by fens is denser and more fibrous. Fens develop where there are slight slopes that remain moist enough for peat to form, but allow a continuous slow flow of water through the peat to carry the nutrients necessary for fen plants. Often fens have a neutral or slightly basic pH, especially those developed on limestone bedrock.

Some fens are poor in nutrients, not much better than bogs, and very few plants grow in them. More interesting are the rich fens with their diversity of flowering plants. Typical orchids of rich fens in the park are the tall showy lady's-slipper and yellow lady's-slipper—both endangered or rare throughout most of their range due to picking and habitat destruction. Accompanying them are such plants as marsh marigold, blue-flag iris, leafy

Yellow pondlily.

Cottongrass.

Purple lousewort.

Grass of Parnassus.

Iris meadow near Sally's Cove.

Kalm's lobelia.

© Michael Burzynski

Rhodora.

© Michael Burzynski

Canada burnet and Joe Pye weed.

© Michael Burzynski

Labrador tea.

© Michael Burzynski

Sheep laurel.

© Michael Burzynski

white-orchis, blue-flowered Kalm's lobelia, glutinous false-asphodel, grass of Parnassus, and meadow rue with its tall white powder puff flower-heads.

PONDS AND LAKES

The waters of the coastal lowland are very different from those on the highlands. They have a higher salt content, darker waters, are better buffered, and are more productive. Organic acids that provide the tint are picked up by the water as it filters through decaying plant matter in peat bogs and forest soils. These are the same acids that colour the decoction of boiled leaves that we call "tea".

Lowland ponds, especially those associated with peat bogs, usually have such dark water that even in knee-deep shallows the bottom becomes invisible. Yellow pondlily, pondweeds, bladderworts, quillworts, bog cotton, and blue-flag iris are the most common plants in and around the ponds. Even small ponds can be whipped into waves by winds blowing over the lowlands. These waves erode the black peat surrounding the ponds, creating half-metre-high peat walls, and small crescent beaches of bleached granite sand on the downwind shore of each pond.

Dragonfly nymphs lurk in the depths. They look like dead leaves, until an insect or small fish comes close enough to be captured and eaten. When necessary, they can expel a jet of water from their abdomens to shoot forward. Brightly coloured adult dragonflies patrol the edges of the ponds, snatching smaller insects from the air with basket-like legs, then killing and eating them in flight. Their two pairs of wings rustle as they maneuver skillfully through the air, clattering in sharp turns and dives, faceted surfaces aglint in the sun like leaded glass. Dragonflies hover as well as any hummingbird, and they have wraparound compound eyes that resemble motorcycle helmets. They can see in almost all directions at once. If a dragonfly will allow you to get close enough, you can literally look deep into its beautiful green eyes—in fact into hundreds of them at a time.

Damselflies are smaller and more delicate relatives of dragonflies. The most common are the tiny bluets. The males are sky blue with black markings, and the females are a warm brown. Their bodies are about the length and thickness of a darning needle, and their wings are as clear as cellophane. They drift along the edges of brooks and ponds in search of tiny flies. Pairs in nuptial embrace dance across the water surface, the male clasping the female behind the head and supporting her so that she can safely deposit her eggs on water vegetation.

Beavers dam most lowland waterways. Their ponds flood across the surrounding land, allowing the beavers to reach feeding areas safely. A system of excavated canals increases their ability to get around without moving far from water. The ponds isolate the beavers' lodges from land predators, and provide a safe storage place for the winter food supply—twigs harvested in the autumn are poked into the mud on the pond bottom, then weighted with

Wallace Brook meanders through Trout River Gulch.

Greg Horne, GMNP

The clear waters of Western Brook.

© Michael Burzynski

stones to provide a winter meal. The bottoms of beaver ponds are excavated deeper and deeper by the beavers as time goes on, since they need the mud to pack holes in the dam.

However, beaver ponds are even more ephemeral than lakes. They are dependent on continuing beaver activity to maintain the dams. When the local food supply is exhausted, beavers leave. Then the dams deteriorate, the water drains away, and the muddy pond bottom becomes an iris swamp and fills in with alders and other floodplain vegetation. Stands of pink-flowered Joe-Pye weed mix with glowing yellow goldenrod, creamy Indian paintbrush, and cleavers. Tangles of willows and cherry trees stand out against the uniformity of the spruce-fir forest. In many cases only low ramparts of half-buried beaver dams hint at the origin of these meadows, and crumbling lodges lie hidden amid dense alder stands.

IRON PANS AND OIL SLICKS

As organic acids accumulate in standing water, bogs, and fens, they leach iron and manganese from the sediments below. These metals have several interesting effects. The rocks along slow-moving streams, beneath peat bogs, and in lowland lakes are often stained orange or shiny purple-black by thin layers of manganese and iron. Bladderworts waving in slow fen streams are sometimes completely encrusted with a rusty film of iron oxide. Iron leached down into the soil can form an impermeable hardpan that impedes drainage, and iron nodules can accumulate through bacterial action at the bottom of bogs. The Norse at L'Anse aux Meadows smelted this iron to forge ship nails.

The most frequently noticed effect of metals in acidic water is the iridescent "oil" slicks that float on puddles in bogs and fens. Often mistaken for natural oil seeps or human spills, these slicks are actually not oil at all. Touch the surface of one lightly, and the colourful slick will shatter. Cracks appear in its surface, and a rain of minute manganese and iron oxide crystals drifts to the puddle bottom. These slicks form when the metals carried in acidic water come in contact with air.

ULTRA-OLIGOTROPHIC WESTERN BROOK POND

Although in Newfoundland a rose may still be a rose, a lake is almost invari-

Jeff Anderson, GMNP

Western Brook Pond as seen from the head of the gorge. Note the tour boat.

Cliffs 600-metres tall line Western Brook Pond.

ably something else. No matter how long or wide or incredibly deep, most bodies of standing freshwater on the Island are called "ponds." In fact, of the thousands of waterbodies in the park—ranging in depth from a few centimetres to "bottomless" Western Brook Pond—not one is called a lake.

Western Brook Pond is a very unusual body of water. It is 16.5 kilometres long and almost 2 kilometres wide at the mouth of the gorge. The Pond is bordered by sheer cliffs that rise up to 670 metres above sea level, and it is 165 metres deep—enough water to submerge a 50 storey office tower. This places its deepest point 135 metres below sea level. Although once a saltwater fjord, the surface of the Pond is now 30 metres above sea level and completely fresh. Only the sea shells and lumps of coralline algae that wash out of its shores belie the Pond's marine past.

Western Brook Pond's water is so free of sediment, organic matter, and human pollution that it is one of the purest lakes in the world. In limnological terms, Western Brook Pond is an ultra-oligotrophic lake. This means that its waters are almost devoid of organic material and nutrients such as phosphorus and nitrogen that plants need; so the Pond can support very few insects, fish, or other animals. To a great degree this is due to the size and character of the watershed that drains into the Pond. The Pond has a surface area of almost 20 square kilometres. Its drainage basin is only about eight times that area—unusual for such a large and deep body of water. About two thirds of the Pond's drainage basin is on the highlands of the Long Range, so it contributes little in the way of sediment or organic matter. The lowland third provides most of the nutrients that are in the Pond.

The waters of Western Brook Pond are clear, deep, and colourless. Its bottom is almost bare of plants, even in the shallows. Although much of the Pond's drainage area is underlain by granitic rock, the water in the Pond has a nearly neutral pH (the water is neither acidic nor basic). Western Brook Pond water is not quite distilled, but natural, organically grown, wild-living, range-fed water does not come much purer than this.

Consequently, there are few fish in this large body of water, although trout and salmon move through it to get from brook to brook. Tour boat operators often see a shadow on their depth sounder that looks like a huge school of fish in the depths of the Pond. A possible explanation is that their sonar is echoing off the steep fjord walls or reflecting from debris at a thermocline—a temperature boundary—and that is why the "fish" are always in the same place.

Gros Morne's boundaries enclose more than a thousand other "ponds," with their accompanying brooks, streams, and rivers. Many thousands of smaller pools and flashets also dot the highlands and lowlands—unnamed and uncounted. Of the park's waterways, 94 watersheds drain directly into the Gulf of St. Lawrence, three flow east before turning to empty into the Gulf (one of these is the Upper Humber River), and only one (the Main River) flows completely east to empty into White Bay on the other side of the Great Northern Peninsula. The Upper Humber River alone drains almost 20% of the park.

River beauty.

Blue flag iris.

Northeastern rose.

Quiet streams are often lined with wildflowers.

RIVERS OF LIFE

Brooks on the lowlands are small, shallow, and relatively slow moving because of the level topography. Their courses are lined with smooth pebbles and boulders, and only occasionally do they spill over bedrock as rapids and low waterfalls. Although the bogs may be nutrient poor, the rivers accumulate and carry nutrients from inland, and are far richer in plant and animal life. Some, such as Western Brook, have wide *steadies* like shallow lakes along their course. Plants root in the muddy bottoms of the steadies, and the warm water becomes a rich feeding area for waterbirds.

As winter's accumulation of snow and ice melts from the land, the major annual erosion event takes place in the park's rivers. Torrents of water rush off the highlands and through the brooks, streams, and rivers of Gros Morne, washing out banks and alluvial terraces, flooding through dry channels, plucking trees from the banks, shifting boulders, gravel, sand, and silt downstream, and reshaping the seasonal structures of each river's course. This is the time of year that brooks look for a new bed, cutting overland to find a faster route to the sea. Meandering streams are common on the lowlands of the park, and some, like Stag Brook, change course almost yearly. They writhe across the landscape in S-curved channels, leaving a trail of abandoned ox-bow ponds in their wake. Abandoned meanders turn into stickleback nurseries, beaver ponds, and eventually rich iris-covered wetlands. New watercourses dig deeply into the gravels, producing dark pools with sandy shallows downstream.

A fast-flowing bouldery section of brook has shallow oxygen-rich water. The rocks will be slippery with brown diatoms and other rock-hugging algae. In rollicking waters, tiny leech-like larvae and hunchbacked pupae of black-flies cling to the downstream side of rocks. The larvae snag fine particles of food from the rushing stream with fan-like appendages. The pupae lie inert,

Indian paintbrush.

Meadow rue.

trailing thread-like gills, quietly changing into their adult form—perhaps dreaming of acres of soft warm skin and meals yet to come.

On the sides of the rocks and underneath is a raucous world where everything is buffeted by roiling currents. Only small plants and animals can cling flat enough to the rock surfaces to avoid the water's pull. Mayfly larvae are streamlined like sports cars, with spoilers built on their bodies to keep them flattened to the rocks. Even their legs and heads are shaped to go with the flow. A millimetre-thin layer of water surrounds each boulder surface, slowed by friction to a relative crawl. It is within this boundary layer that the mayflies, caddisflies, stoneflies, mites, and other invertebrates must live. Any that raises its body too high will be swept away, and consumed by fish waiting downstream. Some caddisflies build centimetre-long tunnels out of tiny stones that they lash together with silk and glue to a boulder's surface. Safe within these strongholds they can trawl for food particles in the flow. Others live in cracks and crevices, and snare meals from the passing flood with small, extraordinarily fine silken nets that they spin. Yet others construct tubular "log cabins" out of tiny sticks, and move about in quieter water in search of food. Flat mayfly larvae skitter over and under the rocks sideways, forwards, and backwards as they search for food.

In rapids, the downstream side of each boulder harbours a quiet zone. Bubbling golden water gushes against the rocks, then eddies around the back. There it slows down and its load of bubbles is released. The silvery spheres rush for the surface of the water, then burst to freedom in a shower of spray. Sand and other pieces of debris settle to the bottom behind the rock, forming a V-shaped tail downstream that marks the deadwater. This is where small trout and salmon parr are often found. They lurk in these pockets of quiet water waiting for insects to be swept past, darting out to retrieve them as they flash by. With a mask and snorkel it is easy to watch these fish feeding and jostling for prime positions, and to see how they rest on the bottom to save energy between meals.

Farther downstream, in shallow riffles, are the mussel beds. Western Brook, Lomond River, and some other streams have sections that are packed almost bank to bank with freshwater mussels. Some of these mussels are as big as a hand, but all that usually shows above the gravel is the gape of the shell where the feeding and waste siphons are exposed to the water. These mussels prefer to live in the fastest currents, and align themselves to the water's flow. The tips of their shells form patterns that graphically illustrate how the water is moving within a stretch of stream.

It is fairly common to find white marine shells on the bottoms of lowland brooks well inland from the sea. Some of these clam, scallop, mussel, and whelk shells look fresh and recent, others are worn and crumbly. In almost all cases they are thousands of years old. They lived in the sea when it covered the lowland all the way to the base of the Long Range escarpment. But eight to twelve thousand years have passed since these animals died, and the lowlands have risen from the sea. Shells buried in streamside mud and gravel deposits are now exhumed and freed to wash to the sea once more.

Streamside tracks tell where moose and caribou have crossed, leaving deeply punched marks in the mud and sand. Bear tracks wander from driftwood to hollow stump to streamside, slowly moving along the brook as the animal plays follow-the-leader with its nose. The large webbed hind feet of beavers leave obvious marks in soft river mud, but these pugmarks pale beside such signs as gnawed stumps, felled logs, stripped twigs, wide dams, muddy canals, bankside lodges, and flooded forest—beavers are not subtle animals. Fox prints barely mar the sand, but where they have scent-marked a stump or boulder, hints of their presence linger pungently in the air. Muskrats leave little piles of chewed grasses and empty freshwater mussel shells. Otters fish in the larger brooks and in ponds, and mink search for fish, insects, and other foods along the streams, leaving tiny tracks that are only recorded in the softest muds, or fresh wet pawprints that evaporate like ghosts on sun-warmed boulders.

Sky-blue belted kingfishers dart above the water, rattling the air with calls that can be heard even above the rush of a stream. Salmon lie dark in the pools, stirring the water with wide tails. They wait for rain and cooler weather that will let them move upstream to the gravel beds where they will dig redds and lay their eggs. Although disease, exhaustion, fishermen, predators, and poachers will take many fish, some will survive spawning to swim downstream and to sea once more.

Spotted sandpipers nest along streambanks, concealing blotchy eggs among the smooth rocks. The adults flutter and bob and peep excitedly when disturbed, flying from rock to rock to lure onlookers away from their nests. Red-breasted mergansers and common goldeneyes nest along the brooks, and strings of ducklings are a common sight, bobbing along behind their mothers as though in tow, or paddling madly, and even hydroplaning along the water surface in a frenzy of spray to escape a real or imagined danger. Canada geese occasionally nest on the lowlands and flocks often land to feed in steadies in the autumn, rising noisily into the air at the slightest suspicion of an intruder. Gulls roost on the open bogs in large numbers, speckling them with discarded white and grey feathers and otherwise providing them with what can be described as an enriching experience.

WATERFALLS

There are hundreds of waterfalls in the park, ranging from small tumbles to narrow vaporous veils that plunge for hundreds of metres. It is hard to think

Bakers Brook Falls.

The Overfalls, south of Trout River Pond.

of a river or brook that does not have a few cascades. The highest waterfalls are along the edges of the great glacial troughs that cut into the Long Range. Most of these falls start at small lakes on the highlands. The water slips over the cliff edge in straight plummeting cascades that fragment into wisps and mists as wind vapourizes the bottom of the plunging water column. Below, the water reorganizes itself into frothing white step-like falls that slowly and carefully wend their way down to the slower brooks on the lowlands. The summit of Gros Morne offers views of a highland waterfall plunging over the cliffs of Ten Mile Pond. Another is seen near the back of Western Brook Pond.

One of the most impressive falls in the park is the Overfalls at the back of Trout River Pond. It pours out of Sandy Pond on the Gregory Plateau, and cascades a hundred metres to the forest below, forming a narrow white stripe down the cliff face. Unfortunately it is not visible from Trout River Pond, but there are places along the backroads where it can be seen.

© Michael Burzynski

Potholes cut into bedrock by a rushing brook.

Where water rushes over bedrock, potholes are cut by rapidly eddying sand and pebbles. On Southeast Brook, some of these potholes are just arm deep, but others beneath waterfalls are so large that their bottoms cannot be seen through the tea-coloured water—one is sunk 13 metres into the bedrock. These were probably cut by glacial meltwater.

EXPLORING THE LOWLANDS

To see the coastal lowlands, try walking some of the following trails: Bakers Brook Falls, Western Brook Pond (which has interpretive signs), Berry Head Pond, and Berry Hill (which offers views over the lowlands). Highway 430 from Rocky Harbour north gives expansive views of lowland wetlands and forest.

Peter Hope, GMNP

Cascade, Bakers Brook Pond.

Cliff on the North Rim of Western Brook Pond.

MOUNTAIN REFUGE

THE HEIGHTS OF THE LONG RANGE LOOK DOWN ON THE rest of Newfoundland. Nowhere else on the Island is there such topography. Gros Morne mountain is the second highest peak on the Island, shorter than Lewis Hill by a mere eight metres. Like the rest of the Long Range, Gros Morne does not fit the usual mental image of the word *mountain*. It is only 806 metres high and has a flat summit. But it rises from sea level, and certainly has a grandeur befitting its name.

The sheer granitic cliffs of the Long Range plateau fall to the waters of Western Brook Pond.

WINTER ON THE HIGHLANDS

The highlands are WHITE in winter: white trees, white animals, white sky, white snow, white ice. Colour drains off the hills some time in November as early snowfalls swathe boulders and plants, and hares and ptarmigan shed summer camouflage in favour of basic white. By mid-December, the only dark things on the highlands are very large erratics, twigs that grew too tall in summer, ravens, and moose. People in bright winter clothing are almost painful to look at in these monochrome mountains. Anything human stands out sharply against the sweeping wind-formed curves, hills, and hollows of snow.

Moose often spend the winter in small groups.

Michael Burzynski, GMNP

Because of the wind, snow on the high country is usually a hard-packed, form-fitting crust—an icy body-cast over the hills. Shard-like snow crystals flurry across the smooth white expanses and rattle against crust and branches. Valleys fill with drifting snow, and landmarks disappear beneath the white blanket. Windblasting around boulders excavates hollows, often exposing bare soil and twig tips. These pits in the snow, called *anjmanja*, are used by rock ptarmigan and Arctic hares for shelter, for feeding, and to obtain digestive grit.

There are few signs of life in the white mantle. Ice-caked tree tops are identifiable by shape rather than by colour. The snow is too hard for tracks, and only frozen droppings mark an animal's passage. Most animals are farther inland, away from the exposed outer hills. Moose congregate to feed in coniferous forest. As they move away from established trails they plunge chest deep into the snow, ploughing and flailing through it in an energy-wasting struggle. Usually they walk in single file in the trees, with a lead animal breaking trail and the others following closely behind. Small herds of caribou move more easily through the white landscape in search of feeding areas. Their wide hooves and lighter weight are better adaptations for winter on the Long Range.

Where blowing snow drifts into highland valleys and hollows, it can accumulate tens of metres deep. This forms the late-melting snowbeds that caribou use as calving areas, and the snow often lasts into August or later. Cornices build up where snow blows over cliff edges, leaving five to ten metres of unsupported drift that later collapses and avalanches downhill. One of the most spectacular of these forms each year at the rim of the cirque bowl above the Tablelands parking lot.

Wind chases plumes of snow across the highlands, stripping exposed heights bare, filling low places, and driving the snow over steep edges and onto the lands below. Even when the lowlands are calm, highland snow seems agitated. It migrates across the hills, and storms over cliffs in clouds. Drifts and swirls of white descend as freak snowstorms out of the blue sky.

Weather on the Long Range is changeable. However, a few things can be counted on: Winds are often strong, with an *average* wind speed between 30 and 45 kilometres per hour, and much stronger during storms. The highlands are usually colder and cloudier than the lowlands, and this has led to the development of tundra rather than boreal forest. Low summer and winter temperatures, shallow wind-blown snow, wind desiccation, and abrasion by blowing ice crystals keep growth low, and the short summer season, high precipitation and meagre soils reduce the number of species that can survive on the hills.

There is little difference between today's Long Range highlands and the glacier edge here 12,000 years ago. Conditions have not changed much, and relict plants remain in control of this difficult terrain. This is especially true of the late snowbed areas, or *zabois*, that provide an arctic microhabitat for some of rarest plants in Gros Morne.

LATE SNOWBEDS

North-facing hillsides on the Long Range are cooler and more sheltered from the sun than other exposures. Snow that accumulates in winter is protected from summer's heat, and hangs like miniature glaciers on valley walls. These late snowbeds are very important habitats for some rare plants, and for the park's woodland caribou.

These snowbeds offer protection from biting and parasitic flies and keep the caribou cool in the warmer days of spring and early summer. Caribou feed around the snowbeds and return to them to rest and chew their cud. Hair, urine, and droppings accumulate on the snow, and wash out as the summer proceeds, fertilizing the plants that grow around the snowbed edges. In this way caribou enrich these favoured calving and feeding areas, and help to support a wide variety of unusual plants that can tolerate the extremely short growing season. Fresh sprouts appear almost daily as the edges of the snowbeds melt back and expose more soil to the warmth of the sun—a handy supply of highly nutritious, easily digestible young leaves that is especially important for calves.

Caribou warble-fly and the caribou nose-botfly are large hairy flies that resemble bumblebees. In Gros Morne and other parts of the Long Range, the late snowbeds are perfect resting grounds for caribou, since these large parasitic flies find it difficult to fly in the cooler air over the snow. These flies disrupt caribou's foraging, ruminating, sleep, and travel, and can have a major effect on the health of animals that do not have recourse to

Overlooking Ten Mile Pond, near the end of the Long Range Traverse.

© Michael Burzynski

Sheldon Stone, GMNP

© Michael Burzynski

Looking into Ten Mile Gulch.

Rest stop near the top of Western Brook gorge.

snowbeds. In large numbers these parasites can cause the death of calves. In August, if the snowbeds have melted, caribou climb onto the highest knolls, seeking breezes to cool them and to keep the flies away. Sometimes ten or twenty crowd together, forming an antlered crown on a hillock. The mass of caribou resembles a branchy clump of tuckamore, except for the snorts and head shakes.

Signs of caribou are everywhere on the highlands: droppings, tracks, and wide trails that lead from one favourite feeding ground to the next on the highlands. Wet soil is sometimes trampled into a quagmire where the animals pass frequently.

Most plants of late snowbed areas are perennial species that are found in the Arctic. They include dwarf willowherbs, mountain sorrel, sibbaldia, brook saxifrage, least willow, purple mountain-heather, and white mountain heather. There are also smooth patches of emerald moss, spiky clubmoss, fern clumps, and mats of grass and sedge. Canada geese visit the late snowbeds in autumn as they fly south through the park, and feed on the greenery, eating berries, seeds, leaves and starchy rhizomes. Goose droppings are commonly seen by hikers on the Long Range. They look like discarded cigar butts, often stained royal blue with crowberry juice.

The least willow is probably the most-northerly-growing shrub in the High Arctic. On the late snowbeds of the Long Range it grows as pairs of tiny glossy leaves enfolding male or female catkins, barely poking out of the moss and lichens. Its slender woody stems creep along underground, showing only buds at the surface in winter. It looks more like a herb than a shrub. Like most of the late-snowbed plants, it has an extremely short life cycle. It must break dormancy, leaf out, produce catkins, achieve fertilization, ripen seeds, store up energy for winter and spring, and then produce next year's buds and shut down its leaves between the time that the snowbed melts out and the first hard frost.

ICE ON THE ROCKS

Frost-shattered felsenmeer is typical of the highest parts of the Long Range, and has led to suggestions that some plants and animals may have survived the most recent glaciation in unglaciated highland *nunataks* (from the Inuit term meaning "ice-free peak projecting through glacial ice"). Recent dating of the weathered surfaces of erratic boulders in nunatak areas indicates that these fields of fractured stone probably were ice covered during glaciation, but the ice was frozen tightly to the ground. Since this "cold-based" ice cannot slip over the surface, it accumulates as snow piles up, then later melts away with minimal disturbance to the ground below. The park highlands were probably islands of white stationary ice surrounded by moving glaciers decorated with brown racing stripes of rock debris. Mosses, and other small plants and animals, may have survived on the steepest portions of the mountain fronts where snow could not accumulate in any quantity during the winters.

HIGHLAND WETLANDS

Lakes fill most depressions on the Long Range plateau. Some flood deep troughs, others lie in shallow rocky bowls, and still others are mere puddles in the peaty wetlands. From the air, the glint and flash of standing water is one of the most memorable features of the highlands. Almost sterile because of lack of nutrients, their water is clear, and their bottoms are almost devoid of plants. Large rounded boulders loom from their depths and litter their rims and the surrounding landscape—standing exactly where the melting glaciers dropped them. Isolated fish that live in these ponds are dwarfed by the lack of nutrient and water conditions. Elsewhere, strings of sparkling lakes carry runoff through glacial valleys, steps on the way down to the sea. Like watery beads strung along a brook, these water bodies are called *paternoster lakes*—after the "Our Father" prayer marked by a rosary bead.

Many wet valleys on the Long Range have filled with a peaty soil as the remains of moisture-loving mosses, grasses, sedges, and shrubs accumulated into peaty bogs and fens. There are four main topographic difficulties faced by hikers on the Long Range: hills to be climbed, lakes and ponds to be circled, wetlands to be waded, and tuckamore to be avoided. The wetlands are a very large part of the Long Range experience, and hikers quickly become adept at sizing up the softness of the ground, which grassy tussock might support weight, and which patch of black muck will suck their boots

Long Range hiker exploring near Hardings Pond.

deep into the mire. There is a style of walking, common throughout Newfoundland, that is used on both highlands and lowlands. This "wetland waddle" is employed when hikers are forced to straddle a wet moose path or other long narrow puddle along a tight wooded trail. To do this you stride along wide legged and assured, one foot on either side of the quagmire. This works wonderfully until a toe snags a root, or the puddle becomes wider than your pelvis will allow. Then you discover how deep the muck is.

HOME ON THE TUNDRA

Visually, and in terms of plant and animal life, the open barrens of the Long Range could be Arctic tundra. Cushion plants grow among the felsenmeer blocks on exposed high barrens. Most common on the granites and quartzites of the Long Range is diapensia. This plant forms tight cushions of green to wine-red leaves, and sends up white flowers to attract bumble-bees and other insects. It carpets parts of Gros Morne's summit, and is common on most other highlands, except where there is limestone or peridotite. The low cushion shape keeps it close to the ground where wind and blowing ice cannot harm it.

When a cushion of diapensia or some other highland plant grows too tall, it leaves the protection of the ground. Snow blows off it in winter, exposing it to the drying wind. No matter how deep its taproot reaches, no water will be available in the frozen soil, and the plant will die. It is not uncommon to find that the centres of the largest diapensia domes are brown and dead.

There are fewer species of breeding birds on the highlands than on the lowlands. They include rough-legged hawks, greater yellowlegs, least sand-pipers, American pipits, American tree-sparrows, white-crowned sparrows, horned larks, common redpolls, willow ptarmigan, and rock ptarmigan. The

Northern violet.

Oxyria, or mountain sorrel.

last two not only raise their young there, but live on the highlands all year. Ravens and robins are frequent visitors.

Another important inhabitant of the highlands is the Arctic hare. They are restricted to the Long Range barrens, and, like ptarmigan, they depend on colour to camouflage them in both summer and winter. The winter coat is completely white, except for black ear tips, and dark eyes. The hair on the underside of their feet is yellowish, but it only shows when they move. In spring, when the snow is patchy and the hares are still white, they will dart onto snowbeds rather than try to hide in tuckamore. As they feed on willow branches in spring, their mouths are sometimes stained brown with the resinous bud coating.

Even in open boulder fields these hares rarely run away, but stay stock still and imitate the rocks around them. Hikers on the highlands stopping for lunch are often startled when a nearby "boulder" starts to move. In winter these hares scrape through the snow crust to reach twigs and buds, and seem

Alpine Willowherb.

Sibbaldia.

Diapensia.

Least willow.

able to eke a living out of even the most inhospitable ice-covered boulder pile in an entire landscape of white. How many Arctic hares live in the park remains unknown; one estimate puts the population as high as several hundred. Because of their rarity and the importance of protecting them, Arctic hares are one of the symbols of Gros Morne National Park.

Solifluction lobes are prominent and often active on the slopes of the higher hills in the park, such as Gros Morne and the Lookout Hills. They are large bulges of soil sagging downslope, held back by a net of vegetation. The top of these bulging masses of soil is usually unvegetated rock rubble, and they sometimes form clusters like flabby steps strewn down the side of a hill. They form in much the same way as patterned ground, but instead of the particles becoming sorted as they thaw, the whole sheet of sodden soil flows slightly. The result is a downhill creep or bulge. Vegetated lobes are stable, those with a rocky front are active.

Alpine azalea.

Mountain cranberry, or partridgeberry.

Purple mountain-heather.

White mountain-heather.

Ice-deposited erratics shelter small plants and animals on the highlands.

Alpine fern.

Mountain clubmoss.

Snowbed moss.

Rock ptarmigan panting in summer heat.

Caribou shedding winter coat, Tablelands.

Sometimes the snow melts before Arctic hares have shed their winter coats.

Large patterned ground rings on Gros Morne mountain.

Sheldon Stone, GMNP

There are deep pits and hummocks of frost-patterned ground in the felsenmeer areas of the Long Range, but in many places this is probably a "fossil" feature—one that is no longer active. The patterned ground atop Gros Morne mountain, for example, takes the form of large rimmed pits. Most of the upper surfaces of quartzite blocks in these pits are covered with slow-growing lichens. Because they must grow on stable rocks, and quickly die if the rocks are rolled over, the lichen on Gros Morne must have remained undisturbed for hundreds of years. Small frost boils on parts of the mountain churn up fresh sandy particles, so there is still some frost action.

Outer surfaces of granitic erratics on the highlands have weathered during millennia of exposure to air, frost, and moisture. White quartz sand and a paste of decayed feldspar (*grus*) accumulate in depressions and around the bases of these ancient rocks. Where boulders are covered by vegetation, soil acids bleach the granite completely white. Strong winds sometimes flip up the corners of peaty soil blankets, exposing the pale rock beneath.

North-facing slopes and cliffs along the edges of the park's glacial lakes harbour some of the rarest flowering plants, ferns, and mosses in Newfoundland. Along with snails, flightless beetles, and lichens, these may hold clues to the history of Newfoundland's plant and animal life during glaciation.

AEOLUS RULES!

Newfoundland is the windiest province in Canada, and winds are particularly strong in Gros Morne—a consequence of the magnificent topography of the Long Range. The glaciated troughs funnel winds onto the lowlands, and cold air flowing off the plateau gains speed as it pours downhill. Wind rattles leaves from bushes and shakes branches out of trees. It lofts waterfalls into a fine mist and tumbles loose rocks from clifftops. Wind floats ravens for hours on motionless .

wings, goads grit into stinging swarms, and heaves waves at headlands. Wind is air made tangible, air made destructive, air empowered as sculptor of vegetation and dune. The wind moulds life all along this coast.

A 1982 easterly wind smashed a picture window in a house in Norris Point, then proceeded to shift the house off its foundation, remove the roof, flatten the walls, and distribute its contents over a wide area. The only things left standing were a toilet and a television set. A mattress was later found at Woody Point, and a large portion of wall was towed in from the mouth of Bonne Bay. The roof had been impaled on a nearby hydro pole, and only one chair from a heavy wooden dining room set was ever located. Incredibly, there were no injuries. A house in Sally's Cove has twice blown off its foundation—ending up tangled in a fence in 1996.

Something special happens over the surface of Western Brook Pond, at the mouth of Bonne Bay, and in other deep glacial valleys when winds flood down off the highlands. As the cold highland winds meet slower-moving lowland air, gusts slam into the Pond surface, lifting curtains of water that drift about like ghostly sailing ships. Sometimes the curtains are whipped into vortices—slowly spinning funnels of air and water. These water devils spin off over the surface of the ponds and bays, spraying up more water or snow as they go. Often there are several of these miniature whirlwinds swirling about and almost bumping into one another like children's tops. A helicopter pilot has estimated the height of a water devil on Western Brook Pond at 260 metres. This phenomenon is sometimes called *white drift* in Woody Point. Rogue winds at the mouth of Western Brook gorge have destroyed a bridge, damaged a building, and lifted a 14 tonne boat. Thankfully, these are rare events.

EXPLORING THE HIGHLANDS

Burridges Gulch Lookoff, in the Southeast Hills, interprets a hanging valley surrounded by barren rock knobs and a scattering of highland erratics. The Lookout Trail is a short hike onto the most accessible part of the highlands with a wonderful panorama. Gros Morne Mountain Trail takes a full day, and is the major highlands experience offered by the park. The two traverses cross large portions of the highlands, but there are no trails.

Dwarfed larches and alders grow from the mantle rock of the Tablelands.

A WORLD APART

ETWEEN STEPHENVILLE AND BONNE BAY ON Newfoundland's west coast lie four flat-topped massifs ranging from 700 and 815 metres high: the Lewis Hills, the Blow-me-Down Hills, North Arm Mountain, and the Tablelands in Gros Morne National Park. These hills are a completely different rock type from the surrounding land. Peridotite is the most important rock type, and freshly broken surfaces are dark olive-green. Some naturally polished blue-green slabs resemble shards of celadon porcelain. Other boulders show a peculiar green and white pattern like reptile scales, an alteration pattern that gives the rock its name: *serpentinite*.

This mass of rock was shifted from the mantle beneath Iapetus Ocean to its present position during a continental collision some 450 million years ago. At the earth's surface this mantle rock is unstable, and weathers quickly. Its decomposition produces very unusual soils on which few plants are able to live. Flat topped and almost barren, this heap of ochre-coloured rock is the single most important geological site in the park. Its scenery is so unlike anything else in the Atlantic Provinces that it almost defies description.

Displaced cross sections of oceanic crust and upper mantle are not very common on the earth's surface. Where these ophiolites occur they are often strongly altered. However, the peridotite of the Tablelands is still relatively unchanged and unvegetated. The rock probably still looks fresh because it was buried beneath other sediments that protected it, and was not completely exposed to weathering until peneplanation and later glaciation exhumed it.

© Michael Burzynski

Hiker on the Tablelands, near Fox Point Brook.

The Tablelands (on the right) as seen from the lookoff near Woody Point.

PERIDOTITE TO SERPENTINITE

Peridotite weathers from dark green to a rusty brown on the surface as oxygen reacts with the iron in the rock. Deeper in the Tablelands, as ground water slowly drains through cracks, a different chemical alteration of the rock occurs. Calcium is released from the peridotite and carried away in the water. The altered peridotite is softer, and is called serpentinite. It forms thin seams along cracks in the bedrock. Swelling slightly, serpentinite seals its cracks off from further water percolation and effectively slows further serpentinization of the surrounding rock. As the face of the Tablelands is shattered by frost, chunks of rock break loose and tumble down its flanks. These boulders crack along their serpentinized layers, and the scale-like pattern of serpentinite is exposed. In places where there was movement along small faults in the Tablelands, the soft serpentinite is smeared into smooth glossy lumps that crumble loose from the surrounding rock. The colour ranges from dark bottle-green to green-blue.

The most important minerals in Tablelands rock are olivine and pyroxene. The ratio of these two minerals is used to differentiate the rocks. Olivine is fine grained and glassy green-black on broken surfaces. Pyroxene is usually seen as coarse crystals scattered through the olivine, or as jagged layers resembling surgical scars. Since olivine is one of the least stable minerals in the weathering conditions of the earth's surface, exposure to water and air quickly alters its chemistry. The speed with which olivine erodes shows in the rounded surfaces and hollows of peridotite boulders. On some rocks, olivine weathers away leaving crystals of pyroxene standing proud of the rock surface. Boots do not last long in the Tablelands: pyroxene crystals are great for traction, since the sharp crystals grip the soles of boots, but they can also slice through leather and skin.

Shrubby cinquefoil.

Debris chutes scar the flanks of the Tablelands.

Black chromite crystals speckle some Tablelands rock. Chromite is the source of chrome used to harden steel and to decorate cars. Although there was much prospecting for commercial deposits before the park was established, no large quantities have ever been found.

MORE THAN JUST ROCK

With so little vegetation, the Tablelands is a textbook of glacial and postglacial features. Many are visible along Highway 431 through Trout River Gulch: the ancient peneplain surface, tors, an old lateral moraine, terminal moraines, cirques, glacial troughs, erratics, rock glaciers, a roche moutonnée, and nivation hollows that still hold snow into summer. Some of the other geomorphological features there are debris chutes with high levees, massive alluvial fans, patterned ground, solifluction lobes, hyperalkaline springs with travertine deposits, thick calcrete layers, late snowbeds, rock slumps, and an outwash terrace.

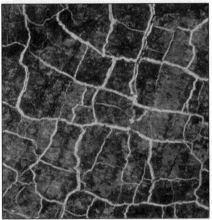
A snakeskin pattern develops in serpentinized cracks.

Serpentinized peridotite.

Tablelands boat tour passing through the Narrows.

Crossing an ice bridge in spring.

The Tablelands has been described as looking like a desert, but there is lots of water out there. It trickles just below the surface wherever there is patterned ground or a field of coarse rock. Water hurtles off the plateau after a rain, since there is almost no vegetation to slow its movement. Crystal-clear streams flow in small steep valleys throughout the year—even during a drought. There is not much living in the streams, however, since there is so little input of organic nutrients. In the Tablelands there are many well developed wetlands. The lower peaty fens are small, but on top of the plateau there is an extensive string fen—a wetland that looks completely out of place nestled into the surrounding rock barrens.

WINTER

Winters are hard in the Tablelands. Snowfall is heavy, and winds are frequently strong. The height and condition of vegetation indicates the average snow depth. Wind sweeps the top of the Tablelands almost bare, and in places rocks show through all winter. In winter there is even less shelter on top than there is in summer, since hollows become packed with snow. The snow drifts into valleys, and is blasted off the plateau top in swirls that turn Trout River Gulch into a veritable snow globe. Trout River Gulch is one of the windiest places in the park, winter and summer. Even when no snow is falling from clouds anywhere in the park, the wind can whip snow in the gulch into white-out conditions that make driving almost impossible. Snowploughs work continuously some days just trying to keep the road to Trout River clear, and high snowbanks build up on either side, almost turning the road into a gully.

Where snow gusts off the top of the plateau, cornices build up. These shelves of hard-packed snow extend out from the upper edges of cirques and cliffs until they are so large that they capsize under their own weight. Small avalanches are not uncommon here. Snow is reluctant to leave the Tablelands even in summer, and patches sparkle from north-facing hillsides into August. If the summer is cool and not too wet (rain melts the snow faster than warm air) the largest of these patches can persist into the next winter. These snowpatches are like proto-glaciers, just waiting for a string of cold years that will let them grow, slide, peel away the underlying rock, and carve their own little cirque valley like Winterhouse Gulch.

As the snow in the cirques melts out from above, brooks beneath the snow, swollen with runoff, cut tunnels from below. Sections of snow collapse or melt away, leaving icy arches over the water. Waterfalls swell, pouring from valley walls into streams that dry out completely as summer progresses. Summer is delayed near the snowpatches, and hikers climbing up to the cirques walk back into spring. The plants that grow in these late snowbed areas must be able to grow and flower quickly. Recent botanical research has shown that most of the plants in the Tablelands late snowbeds—are the same as those that grow around the Long Range snowbeds despite the great difference in rock types.

LIFE ON THE MANTLE

Plants are well adapted to living in the soils that develop from crust rock, but have had little experience with the combination of minerals found in the mantle rock. Some of the elements that plants need most are nitrogen, potassium, phosphorus, and calcium. These are all uncommon in the mantle rock of the Tablelands. However, nickel, magnesium, cobalt, iron, and chromium are abundant enough to be toxic to many plants.

To add to those drawbacks, the serpentine barrens have unstable slopes, hyperalkaline groundwater, extensive frost churning and soil flow, and severe climatic conditions. The soil is really just a rocky rubble with particles ranging from clay to large boulders. It is not an ideal growth medium for plants.

Even though they have both been ice free for the same length of time, there is very little vegetation on the Tablelands compared to the forested crustal rock on the opposite side of Trout River Gulch. Although the Tablelands may look like a 720-metre-high gravel pile, it is far more interesting than any other part of the park. This vast expanse of ochre-coloured rock is spattered with tiny islands of green. One plant that grows here is only found on serpentine soils throughout North America. It is a chickweed rel-

Marcescent-leaved sandwort, a serpentine endemic.

Alpine campion.

Seaside thrift.

ative with star-shaped white flowers and needle-like leaves, called marcessent-leaved sandwort for the way that its dead leaves cling to the stems. Other plants are not restricted to serpentine soils, but are only found here in the park: maidenhair fern, alpine campion, and Lapland rosebay. A third group is associated with both serpentine and limestone soils in the park: trailing juniper, common juniper, seaside thrift, small-flowered anemone, yellow mountain-saxifrage, purple saxifrage, and balsam ragwort.

There are a few black spruce trees atop the plateau, but they are contorted and stunted. Sedges, mosses, arctic-alpine plants, and junipers spring up here and there in the shelter of boulders. The most characteristic moss is grey wool moss. It grows slowly, and forms large clumps—some so big that they resemble sheep wedged in cracks between boulders. Dull grey when dry, this moss turns bright green when wet, and even a light mist is enough to enliven it. Exposed stems look like tangles of black horsehair, and dead clumps are sometimes mistaken for the charred remains of old campfires.

Lower down there are more trees. Black spruce and eastern larch are common, with balsam fir, green alder (often called *mountain alder* in Newfoundland), and even a few white pine. All of these are stunted depending on the amount of shelter. The lack of nutrients and exposure to high winds deform these trees and slow their growth, but do not stop them from producing seeds—unlike the stunted spruce and fir of the Long Range highlands. White pines are not common in the Tablelands, and suffer badly from the conditions. Some tower a full 150 centimetres high, with trunks almost 30 centimetres in diameter. They bear normal sized cones on branches only knee-high. These dwarf trees range in age from 80 to 150 years. Strangely, the Tablelands seems to be the one of the few places in the park where white pine seedlings are surviving and growing.

Even smaller and older than these little trees are the junipers (to confuse things, eastern larch is called *juniper* in Newfoundland; in other parts of Canada it is usually called *tamarack* or *hackmatack*). Both common juniper and trailing juniper grow on the peridotite barrens. Common juniper has stiff stems and spiny foliage, while trailing juniper grows scaly leaves and sprawls across the ground with flexible vine-like branches.

Winds that roar through Trout River Gulch during the summer are just the mild-mannered cousins of the storms of winter. In winter, insulating snow is blasted away from any exposed sites and collects in deep drifts in hollows. Plants are bared to the drying wind and sun, to cold, and to abrasion by wind-borne ice and sand particles. Branches and buds that poke through the meagre snow cover are quickly pruned back. This shapes the vegetation so that dense cushion mounds and tiny contorted trees are the characteristic forms on these barrens. Junipers growing in the most open sites are wind pruned to the extent that they seem to creep among the rocks. Some with trunks only a couple of centimetres across have more than 300 growth rings.

Because of all the bare rock the Tablelands looks like a desert—but there is rarely a shortage of water. Most plants will draw water from the soil year round. However, in winter when the soil is frozen, plants suffer from desiccation, and that is the most dangerous time of year for the small trees. Resins protect their meagre trunks from fungal and bacterial decomposition, but

Lapland rosebay.

Harebell and pearly everlasting.

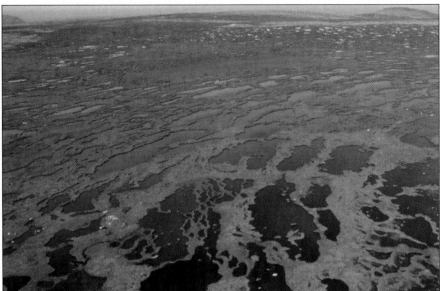

String fen on top of the Tablelands plateau.

winter flays these tiny trees by sunburning and drying their thin bark. Dead bark is stripped away by wind-driven ice and sand grains, exposing and eroding the wood until only a bleached keel is left. This is enough to shelter a shred of live cambium that keeps the crown alive, but the tree cannot add a ring of new wood and bark each year—only a strip. Uneven growth may also explain the twisted trunks of many of these trees. Some of these horizontal trees have seven-metre trunks, but because they lie flat, their actual height is only 10 centimetres.

Remarkably, these junipers do not just survive, they thrive. Most of them have enough energy to produce a heavy crop of berries each summer. Actually fleshy cones, these "berries" start out green, then turn powdery blue, and eventually black. When crushed they release the fragrance that made them famous, and gives them the name gin berries.

Elsewhere in Canada, maidenhair fern grows in hardwood forests. In Gros Morne it is almost impossible to find a hardwood forest, let alone one with ferns in it. The fine black stems of maidenhair are glossy, and look fragile and brittle; its finely divided leaves seem appropriate for a tropical plant shading a languid jungle pool. But in the Tablelands, robust clumps of maidenhair ferns jut right out of the boulders along streams, usually where they are sheltered somewhat from the winds. Likewise, on the mainland, royal fern forms thickets in rich floodplain soils, where it unfurls fronds two or even three metres tall. On peridotite, however, royal fern is somewhat less regal, and its fronds rarely exceed 30 centimetres. Translucent as they unfold in spring—glowing red with the sun behind them—they become light green in summer, and turn bright yellow and orange with the cold nights of autumn.

Tablelands rocks rarely show any sign of lichen growth, save for ghostly white rings that seem barely alive. An exception are bright orange patches of lichens on boulders frequently used as perches by birds, boulders that have been heavily fertilized. The metals in the peridotite probably inhibit lichen growth, and the fact that the surface of peridotite is less chemically stable than quartzite or granite means that slow-growing lichens would slough off as the rock disintegrates. Erratics sprinkled among the ochre peridotite are different. These rocks, carried from elsewhere by glaciers, have lain around for the same length of time as the Tablelands rocks, and are usually completely encrusted with yellow, grey, and brown lichens.

Anyone who has spent any time in a bog knows about the insect-eating pitcherplants. But anyone accustomed to seeing pitcherplants in bogs and fens will be surprised to find them growing in wet gravel, and popping out of cracks in cliffs in the Tablelands. These plants do not actually eat insects; they just trap them in their red-veined hollow leaves. There the insects drown in rainwater that collects in the leaves, and they are broken down by a disassembly crew of insects, rotifers, and bacteria. The plant merely absorbs the molecular remains. Pitcherplants trap spiders, snails, slugs, centipedes, and anything else that tries to explore their leaves. The plants benefit from the

© Philippe Henry

Greater yellowlegs nest in the Tablelands fens.

Grey wool moss sometimes outgrows common juniper

Lichen-covered erratic in the middle of a peridotite barren.

nitrogen and other nutrients that they get from their prey—nutrients that are in short supply in the depauperate soils of bogs and the Tablelands.

Pitcherplants are not the only carnivorous plants in the Tablelands. In fact, this part of the park seems to be a veritable death trap for insects. Everywhere there are nutrient-starved plants out for a bit of fresh meat. In pools lurk trailing tufts of bladderworts sprinkled with tiny traps triggered by motion. Yellow butter-pale leaves are the business end of the butterwort, and their upper surfaces are covered with moist glands that trap prey. Several species of red sticky-leaved sundews also live in wet places. All of these plants supplement the meagre pickings from the soil by consuming animals— fair turnabout for all those millions of years of animals eating plants.

Shrubby cinquefoil and Canada burnet grow everywhere in the Tablelands. The first is a bush that rises almost knee high and starts to bear its bright yellow flowers early in the summer. Blooming continues until the frost. The second prefers wetter sites, and grows a tall stalk of white bottlebrush flowers in late summer. Balsam ragwort also has yellow flowers, but they look like emaciated dandelions. It grows throughout the lowlands, often mixed with clumps of nodding blue harebells. Yellow mountain-saxifrage has fleshy leaves and orange-spotted yellow flowers, and is common in wet gravels throughout the lowlands.

There is not much animal life in the Tablelands. Caribou use the valley on the western end of the plateau, and are occasionally seen in Trout River Gulch, as are moose. Rock and willow ptarmigan live on the plateau top, but are rarely encountered. Ants are everywhere. It is difficult to know what

James Steeves, GMNP

Bicoloured gravels at the Narrows, Trout River Pond.

they are all eating, but they seem to do well in the gravelly soil. Their hills are easy to find since they are usually a bit darker than the surrounding soil, and all of the rock particles that the ants have excavated and mounded up are much the same size—just right for a single ant to handle. Grasshoppers leap wildly and sometimes spread black and yellow wings to flee danger.

Spiders are also common. Wolf spiders scurry among the rocks, legs long enough to span a dollar coin. Some females carry egg cases that look like tiny golf balls. Elsewhere there are large jumping spiders that leap on prey rather than building webs. They are the only spider that will turn their "head" to look at the person who is observing them. One of their four pairs of eyes is greatly enlarged, and there is a real owl or cat look to the "faces" of these tiny fuzzy predators. Tiger beetles are also predators, with long legs, large mandibles for grasping prey, and a couple of light stripes on their wing cases. They race across the ground looking for smaller insects, and take rapidly to flight if approached. When they raise their wing cases to fly, their emerald bodies sparkle in the sun. There are other predatory beetles in the Tablelands, and some plant eaters.

SOIL MOVEMENTS

In unvegetated rock rubble, ice expansion pushes particles of rock apart from each other, heaving the ground slightly. During a thaw, the ground slumps back down, and small particles fill the spaces between larger ones. This eventually sorts the rubble into a network of rock rings with gravelly centres. On the surface of the barrens this pattern of frost boils looks like a honeycomb or net: small boulders form the roughly hexagonal "mesh," and mounds of gravel and sand fill the "holes." This is *patterned ground*, also known as *stone rings*, *frost boils*, and *frost polygons*. The rings are sometimes several metres across. On gentle slopes, the polygons become stretched and form *stone*

Stone rings.

Stone stripes.

stripes. Patterned ground is typical of the Arctic and of alpine terrain, and of periglacial (near glacier) conditions. It depends on deep freezing—below one metre—for its formation. Trout River Gulch may be one of the most southerly places in Canada to see this feature near sea level.

The rings and stripes of patterned ground around the base of the Tablelands determine where plants can grow. Active stripes are usually barren, probably because seedlings are regularly churned out of the soil before they can grow deep roots. Larger stone rings usually have plants in the centre, but nothing growing in the well drained rocks around the edge. The network formed by interconnected stone rings actually seems to produce a complex drainage channel for these patterned soils, and even after a heavy downpour there is no sign of surface runoff—no disturbance of the plants and finer material in the centres of the rings—but the sound of trickling water is everywhere.

The centre of these rings is composed of a plug of sand and clay that goes down a metre or more. Once plants have sunk a strong taproot into this, they seem fairly secure. In some places the centres of these stone rings are sunken, offering a modicum of wind protection for plants that grow in them. In other places—such as the top of the Tablelands—they are domed, and although plants can use the soil, they are more exposed to wind and abrasion.

View down on Trout River Pond.

© Michael Burzynski

Moss campion is a typical plant of patterned ground. This deep-rooted plant of the Arctic grows as a compact cushion. Its small glossy leaves are almost hidden in spring by a mass of pink flowers. Another plant of the Tablelands is alpine campion, a serpentine endemic that grows about 20 centimetres tall. It has darker flowers at the top of a stout leafy stem. Grasses and sedges sprout in tufts and clumps, and the succulent leaves of seaside thrift grow in small rosettes. The papery pink flower-heads of seaside thrift

A travertine seep.

look almost like the flowers of chives as they rustle in the wind on thin crooked stems.

GROS MORNE'S ROCK DU JOUR

Although the Long Range is more than a billion years old, Gros Morne also contains rock that is fresher than today's bread. The rock is called travertine, and it looks like light stains on the flanks of the Tablelands, often with lush plant growth. It begins to form when water percolates through cracks in the peridotite of the Tablelands. During its slow passage, the water causes chemical reactions in the surrounding rock. Small amounts of calcium are released by the peridotite bedrock as it turns to serpentinite. The calcium (as calcium hydroxide) is carried away by groundwater and finally bubbles out on the flanks of the Tablelands at springs. The calcium hydroxide reacts with carbon dioxide in the air, producing calcium carbonate, which rapidly precipitates on rocks around the springs. This instant-setting limestone cement forms layers of travertine, cements streamside rubble into natural concrete (calcrete), and is the youngest rock in Newfoundland. Travertine often produces a complex pattern of tiny dams and rims over rock surfaces.

Travertine springs do not flow forever. Eventually the fractures that feed the springs seal up with serpentinite, or the drainage changes with erosion, leaving patches of dry travertine crumbling on the hillsides. The light brown colour of these calcium rich areas contrasts well with the surrounding ochre-coloured rock. Calcium-loving plants grow around the travertine—many of the same plants that grow on limestone cliffs and the barrens north of the park. Most striking are the yellow lady's-slipper orchids. Small clumps of these yolk-yellow flowers peep from the shelter of shrubs and grasses, looking very much out of place in the seemingly sterile serpentine soils. Mountain avens covers the travertine with tight mats of tiny arrowhead

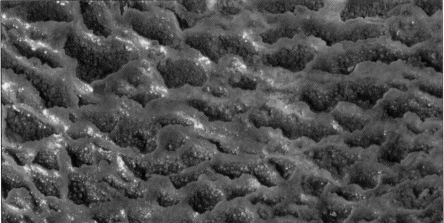

Close-up of travertine surface.

leaves and creamy flowers, and small-flowered anemone produces clumps of white blooms. Elsewhere in the Tablelands there is either not enough calcium for them to survive, or there is too much magnesium, a toxic element taken up by plants in lieu of calcium.

Because there is so little vegetation, it is extremely difficult to judge heights and distances in the Tablelands. What looks like a short, flat, and easy hike can turn out to be a long hard struggle over jumbled boulders.

GREEN GARDENS

Northeast of the Tablelands is the Green Gardens coast. "Green Gardens" is a peculiar name for this part of Newfoundland—it sounds verdant and pastoral, not what one expects for a stretch of cliffs with serious coastal exposure. Surprisingly, Green Gardens *is* idyllically verdant and pastoral (ignoring the odd thistle and nettle—both called *needles* locally).

Green Gardens' rocks are remnants of a volcanic island, and were dragged into place during the emplacement of the Tablelands. Cliffs along the coast there are made up of layers of basalt and pillow lavas. The original glassy surfaces of the pillows have decomposed into a crumbly greenish mass. Water percolating through the rock deposited calcium carbonate and silica in spaces between pillows. White layers built up, and small crystals of calcite and quartz grew, lining some voids and filling others. Red iron oxide and other chemicals colour the veins. The headland beside the staircase is a mass of basalt pillows, and they bulge from the cliffs and intertidal platform almost all the way north to Wallace Brook.

Gasses bubbled out of the flowing molten rock, but as the lava cooled into basalt some bubbles became trapped. The bubbles are preserved to this day as hollow vesicles in the basalt. Percolating water carried traces of min-

Intertidal platform, eroding headlands and a sea stack at Green Gardens.

erals such as calcite that slowly filled some of these vesicles, leaving the dark rock speckled with round white and pink amygdules (named—in Latin—because they resemble almonds in a cake). Elsewhere the basalt shattered as it cooled. The shards were later cemented together with calcite into a striking black-and-white or brown-and-white breccia. Pebbles of breccia and amygdaloidal basalt are polished by the waves, peppering the beach with patterned stones.

Frost wedging and waves in the last few thousand years cut a wide intertidal platform skirting the coast. The cliff base has also been undermined by waves and frost, leaving a clear notch. The intertidal platform is almost flat and is completely covered at high tide. Water has explored lines of weakness between the basalt pillows, excavating some completely. At low tide the platform is exposed, and the potholes and cavities in its surface become rich tidepools to explore for marine plants and animals. Some adjacent potholes have worn through and joined to make larger tidepools, or are connected by holes or small arches.

The cliff rising from the intertidal platform to the meadows is eroded in places into sea caves or grottos. Most are small, but there is a large cave near the southwestern end of the beach. It gapes both high and wide, but cuts only about 15 metres back into the hillside. This cave clearly illustrates how different layers of rock erode at different rates. The volcanic

Sea stack of pillow basalt and tuff.

Sea stack of volcanic breccia.

© Michael Burzynski

J. McCarthy, GMNP

rock layers are tilted so that they are now almost vertical. The outermost rock at the cave is a layer of basalt worn through at one point, creating the mouth of the cave. Behind it is a layer of softer greenish tuff —a rock composed of volcanic ash and shards. It erodes much more easily; thus the high arched chamber is far larger than the mouth of the cave. Rocks in the cave are dangerously slippery—be careful.

Rock pillars and islands line the shore between Trout River and Wallace Brook. Most of these sea stacks are remnants of rock slumps off nearby cliffs. All loose rock has crumbled and washed away, leaving these marine monuments. The largest stack is north of the Green Gardens grotto, and it clearly shows the same layers of pillow lava and tuff that form the grotto. Gulls seem to regard the top of this stack as a particularly safe place to nest.

Coastal meadows at Green Gardens.

Much older stacks rise from meadows high above the seashore. Like The Old Man at the community of Trout River, these were worn by the sea during higher sea level just after glaciation. About 11,500 years ago sea level fell, and the coastal cliffs, the intertidal platform, and the sea stacks were left high and dry. Now the cliffs are hidden in the forest, the intertidal platform is a meadow, and the stumps of raised sea stacks are scratching posts for sheep. One small stack at the far northern end of Green Gardens has a tiny tree growing out of it almost horizontally—a bonsai on a rocky island in a sea of grass.

The lava at Green Gardens is relatively high in calcium, potassium, phosphorus, and other nutrients, and the soil derived from the breakdown of these crumbly volcanic rocks is rich and deep. The soils at Green Gardens grow lush crops of grass, and these coastal meadows have been used for generations as sheep pasture. Small flocks of sheep still graze the fields, climbing right to the top of the precipitous meadows, and also following gullies to the beach to graze on seaweed. Sheep trails wend through the grass and tuckamore. On the steeper slopes, decades of sheep trampling have cut shallow "terracettes" like contour lines around the slopes. These deep soils are prone to landslides and slumping. Gullies have been carved

Sheep still graze in the meadows at Green Gardens.

by runoff, whole hillsides have slipped down towards the sea, and slumping shifts portions of the Green Gardens Trail downward from year to year.

Traces of vegetable gardens are still visible in the grass, close to where there were once summer fishing premises on the beach. Sheep from Trout River find their own way up the coast in spring, and back to the community again in the autumn.

EXPLORING THE TABLELANDS AREA

Three trails cross portions of the Tablelands: Tablelands Trail, a short trail with interpretive signs; Trout River Pond Trail, a long hike across one flank of Table Mountain; and Green Gardens Trail, a complex of trails that starts on Tablelands rock and leads to the shore. Trout River Pond Boat Tour interprets the geology and vegetation of the Tablelands.

Lobster Cove Head Lighthouse.

LIVING ON THE EDGE

T HE PAST LIVES IN MEMORIES. BUT MEMORIES MUST BE kept warm—without repetition they cool and turn to ash. For almost five thousand years people have lived along this coast, each successive culture depending on the sea for transportation and food, each choosing the same sort of place for a home. During those five millennia, each new family that explored this coast has camped on the hearths of earlier folk. Generations have come and gone, and during each lull the grass and tuckamore have crept back, covering tool flakes, campsites, and the cold ashes of the past. Sometimes this coast was alive with hunting and fishing camps. At other times, decades passed with no footprints in the sand and no human voices to disturb the gulls, the caribou, or the seals.

There is no technology to let us visit the past, but there is a magic in the headlands—as though sea breezes stir life into dusty memories. To understand this land, pause awhile in a quiet coastal meadow or hunker down in the tuckamore out of the wind, look out to sea, and let the magic work. Drift off to a past when the forests were new, humans were few, and the scars of the Ice Age still raw....

© Michael Burzynski

Coastal meadow at Trout River.

Maritime Archaic Indian burial mound at L'Anse Amour.

MARITIME ARCHAIC INDIANS—
THE FIRST NEWFOUNDLANDERS

These earliest people are shadows. We know only their bones, their stone hearths, tools, grave goods, and camp waste. We do not know their language, their beliefs, or even their eventual fate. We call these people the *Maritime Archaic Indians*. What they called themselves will always be a mystery. Our sterile label merely defines their preference for coastal sites and dependence on marine resources; their lifestyle, surviving entirely on hunting and gathering wild foods; and their Indian-style tools.

People of this culture lived along the coast of the Maritime Provinces (New Brunswick, Nova Scotia, and Prince Edward Island) and in parts of New England, where their habitation sites and cemeteries are found today. They expanded north on the mainland during the period of climatic warming after the last glaciation. By 9,000 years ago they had populated the coast of Quebec and southern Labrador. The earliest evidence for their fully maritime lifestyle comes from L'Anse Amour in southern Labrador, which is also the site of the oldest known burial mound in the Americas. There, a Maritime Archaic child about 12 years old was carefully buried 7,500 years ago with tools, a bone flute, a walrus tusk, chunks of ochre and graphite, and other materials. The body was laid face down, covered with large slabs of rock, and buried in a large sand tumulus capped with boulders. Who the child was and what precipitated the elaborate burial are mysteries.

This is not an hospitable coast. Here, at the time when people in warmer climes were first experimenting with the wheel, dirtying their fingers with cuneiform writing, and levying the first taxes, the Maritime

Archaic Indians developed a complex technology for hunting and capturing marine mammals, for seasonal travel over expanses of water and snow, and for clothing and shelter in a land where winters are harsh and claim more than half of each lifetime. These people were remarkably successful at what they did, and managed to occupy the coast of Labrador for at least four thousand years—and perhaps longer.

Maritime Archaic Indian tools.

Jean-François Bergeron, Parks Canada

Some 5,000 years ago, bands of these pioneers crossed the Strait of Belle Isle, reaching the Island of Newfoundland either by boat or by trekking over the ice. The major Maritime Archaic site discovered so far in Newfoundland is at Port au Choix, 160 kilometres north of Gros Morne. Families from up and down the west coast probably congregated there for part of the year, then dispersed to their hunting grounds.

The largest known Maritime Archaic Indian burial site in North America is at Port au Choix. These people often decorated their dead with red ochre powder. People were buried with charms, amulets, and pendants;

Different peoples have lived on the Island of Newfoundland at different times, and all have been strongly dependent on the sea.

Mi'kmaq

European Presence

Basques

Norse

Recent Indian Cultures

Dorset Palaeoeskimos

Groswater Palaeoeskimos

Maritime Archaic Indians

| 5000 | 4000 | 3000 | 2000 | 1000 | Present |

Years Before Present

with hunting weapons; and even with large dogs. The careful burial of the dogs makes it obvious that they were valued animals. Although the Maritime Archaic people kept dogs, there is no indication yet that they used them to draw sledges. Cow Head and Norris Point were important locations for these people, and the oldest campsite found so far in the Gros Morne area was used about 4,500 years ago.

They hunted harp seals in the spring, camping along the coast, harvesting other marine life as the summer progressed. Beaches and cliffs were important sources of chert and other rock for tool making. Since most food resources were only seasonally abundant, migration was as much a way of life for these people as it was for their prey. As winter approached they probably moved inland to hunt caribou, beaver, Arctic hare, marten, otter, muskrat, fox, and ptarmigan. They would also find protection from the winter wind. In spring they moved back to the coast to meet the migrating seals.

One of their most sophisticated tools was the toggling harpoon. Attached to a line, it came loose from its shaft when plunged into an animal, and twisted sideways so that it could not pull out of the wound. This held the seal long enough that it could be dispatched. They made many other tools, including heavy gouges that may have been used for making dugout canoes, wooden cooking utensils, or wooden frames for skin boats. Although the Maritime Archaic Indians must have used boats, no remains have yet been found.

Their parka-like clothing was sometimes decorated with shell beads. These people had the tools and skill to produce fine carvings, but only a few stone and bone carvings have survived. The heads of merganser ducks decorate combs, and various birds, mammals, and unrecognizable abstract forms were also used. Their most famous carving in western Newfoundland is a killer whale effigy teased from hard stone. It was found at the Port au Choix cemetery.

Maritime Archaic Indians seem to have developed long trade routes for some raw materials, or traveled great distances to get them. Translucent grey chert from outcrops at Ramah Bay in northern Labrador shows up in Maritime Archaic sites throughout Newfoundland and Labrador, as well as in the Maritimes. Ramah chert seems to have been preferred over local chert for tool making. It is purer and makes a sharper edge than the local clay-rich chert, although their preference may not have been entirely due to the physical properties of the stone.

Perhaps the Maritime Archaic Indians had to depend too heavily on too few prey species and were decimated by several consecutive bad years; perhaps climatic conditions changed too rapidly for them to adjust their hunting and shelter technology; perhaps seal or caribou migration routes were disrupted. Like so many things about these remarkable pioneers, we will probably never know why they declined.

PALAEOESKIMOS, PEOPLE OF THE SEAL

Palaeoeskimos arrived in northern Labrador 4,000 years ago. These very different people had been rapidly moving across the Arctic from Alaska during a warming period about 4,500 years ago, bringing their own technology, lifestyle, language, and beliefs. They used the same resources as the Maritime Archaic Indians, and their southward expansion may have been at the expense of these earlier people. Whatever happened, after millennia of successful settlement the Maritime Archaic Indians disappeared completely from the archaeological record in Labrador within the next 500 years—and were replaced by Palaeoeskimos, often at exactly the same campsites.

Jean-François Bergeron, Parks Canada

Maritime Archaic Indian killer-whale effigy, Port au Choix.

Pre-Dorset Culture—Immigrants from the North

First of the Palaeoeskimos to live in the park area were people of the Pre-Dorset Culture. They arrived on the Island about 3,000 years ago, probably following the harp seals which whelped farther and farther south as the climate cooled. In spring, while seals were whelping, these nomads lived on coastal headlands and hunted out over the ice. They used many of the same raw materials as the Maritime Archaic Indians, and their lifestyle was also quite similar, but they left none of the large woodworking tools that are

NOTEPAD

Palaeoeskimo means prehistoric Eskimo. The term *Eskimo* is used to identify non-Indian inhabitants of the eastern Arctic and Subarctic after the Maritime Archaic Indian period. The term distinguishes them from modern Inuit, who are not their direct descendants. *Inuit* is a name used for non-Indian Arctic peoples since European contact.

Harp seal napping on an ice pan.

© Michael Burzynski

common at the earlier Indian sites. This may indicate that workable wood was less available by the time that they settled here, or just that working wood was not part of their cultural tradition.

Their technology was well adapted for dealing with harsh northern winters and a migratory lifestyle. Their tools were mostly small, sharp, delicate stone blades. Along with harpoons, spears, and lances, they also used the hunting bow.

Groswater Culture

Some 300 years later another Palaeoeskimo group showed up on the park coast—the Groswater Culture. They spread south from Labrador, and their campsites are found along the west and north coasts of the Island of Newfoundland. They also camped where the huge harp seal herds could be intercepted during winter and spring migrations. These people seem to have had a seasonal pattern like the Maritime Archaic Indians. They depended most heavily on marine resources, but also hunted land animals.

They lived in small seasonal camps of a few families. The waste middens that they left show that their diet included harp seals and other seals, seabirds, eggs, small game, fish, and caribou, but there is no indication of whales or walrus being taken. Food was probably eaten raw or cooked in skin containers heated with rocks from the fire pit. Mottled high grade chert from Cow Head (in the park area) or the Port au Port Peninsula was used by the Groswater Palaeoeskimo for tools, and has been found as far away as Killinek in northern Labrador.

Dorset Culture

The most recent Palaeoeskimo people in the park area were the Dorset Culture. About 1,900 years ago they replaced the Groswater people. They may have been a later stage of the Groswater Culture who used slightly different tools, or a completely new group that migrated in from the north. Dorset campsites are on headlands, close to the water's edge. These people specialized in hunting marine mammals, especially the harp seal. They intensely used whatever resources were abundant, and this is reflected in their tools, site location, house construction, and refuse piles. The Phillip's Garden site at Port au Choix covers four hectares, and is much larger than any Groswater sites. In the middens at Phillip's Garden, 98% of the bones are from harp seals.

Whale bone sledge runners have been found at Dorset sites, but no dog bones or harness parts—so the sledges may have been hauled by hand for transporting prey and belongings. The Dorset people lived here until 1,100 years ago, then they too just disappear from the record.

Newfoundland was the southernmost extreme for Palaeoeskimo settlement in North America, and they may have been forced out by uncertain climatic conditions that disrupted the harp seal hunt and the other food sources on which they depended. Without a trustworthy food supply these people would have been extremely vulnerable through the long winters. Perhaps they became extinct, perhaps they retreated to mainland Labrador. Inuit legends says that there were Dorset people in northern Labrador when the Thule immigrants first arrived around 1,000 years ago.

RECENT INDIAN CULTURES

This term encompasses all Indian occupation of Newfoundland since the end of the Dorset Palaeoeskimo period. Unfortunately this occupation is not well represented in the archaeological record of the park, and the people who left the remains are unidentified—they could possibly have been Innu (Montagnais) from Labrador, or their relatives, the Beothuk. There are traces of Indian occupation at Cow Head and Broom Point about a thousand years ago, but so far nothing more recent has been found.

Beothuks

When Europeans arrived in Newfoundland in the 1500s, they met the Beothuks, mostly in the north central and eastern parts of the province. They were the first North Americans encountered by Europeans, and were probably the source of the name "Red Indians" because of their use of powdered ochre for body decoration and painting canoes. Sadly, European disease and expansionism forced the Beothuks farther and farther away from dependable food supplies, and the population declined drastically. Shanawdithit, the last known Beothuk, died of tuberculosis in 1829, and much of what we know of her people comes from her descriptions and remarkable drawings. No indisputable evidence has been found of Beothuks in the park area, although there is a prehistoric site at Port au Choix, and an important Beothuk site was discovered at Deer Lake in 1992.

Mi'kmaqs

The Mi'kmaqs of Nova Scotia, New Brunswick, and Prince Edward Island were one of the first native groups to meet Europeans as the colonization of North America began. It is possible that Mi'kmaqs from Cape Breton visited Newfoundland long before the first European record of their presence on the Island; however, no evidence has yet been found of prehistoric

Matty Mitchell, woodsman extraordinaire, 1919.

settlement. The Mi'kmaqs used large sea-going bark canoes with high gunwales, and later adopted European sailing shallops. Reports mention Mi'kmaqs in Newfoundland as early as 1601, and in the 1670s Mi'kmaq fur trapping parties were reported on the Avalon Peninsula, probably visiting from Cape Breton.

Native woodsmen guided most of the parties exploring the interior of the Island, including William E. Cormack on his cross Newfoundland hike in 1822, and the pioneering geological surveys of Alexander Murray and James Patrick Howley. They later guided for big game hunters and fishermen. One of the best known of these woodsmen was Matthew (Matty) Mitchell. He was born in 1850, either in Norris Point or Halls Bay. He was the son of King Mitchell, an early chief in the Bonne Bay area. A hunter, trapper, lumberjack, prospector, and well-known guide, his most important discovery was the large copper-lead-zinc ore body that he found in 1905 with Will Canning. It later became the Buchans Mine.

Today headlands are the abode of ghosts. Unlike European settlers, the earliest peoples of this coast lived on the wild capes. They could look out over the jumbled pack ice of spring or over the cold waves of early summer and watch for signs of life. Their homes were temporary because they had to move throughout the year to find the seals, the caribou, the fish and birds, and the wild fruit that they depended on. Seals were one of the most important animals in their lives, and marine fish were probably only a minor item in their economy. But a new people was coming, a people with very different ideas about fish and seals.

Reconstructed Norse sod huts at L'Anse aux Meadows.

EUROPEANS

There are legends of earlier visitors, but the first Europeans to live along this coast—and in the whole of the Americas—were Norse. They came here for timber, food, and furs about five hundred years before the age of European exploration, and even then they found a land already long occupied.

Viking means "pirate" or "raider," and is not really an appropriate term for these explorers. The first Norse known to have seen North America were Bjarni Herjolfsson and his crew in 986, blown off course during a trip from Iceland to the Greenland settlement. His accounts of forested coast led Leif Eiriksson to explore with a crew of 35, and around the year 1000 made several landings along the coast.

Interior of a sod hut.

Basque tile sherds at Red Bay.

© Michael Burzynski

Eiriksson's return to Greenland the next year with timber and fruit was the beginning of a series of expeditions and attempted settlements of the new land that they called *Vinland*. Within a few decades, though, internal disputes, hostilities with the natives (*Skraelings* to the Norse), and worsening climatic conditions hastened the Norse abandonment of North America. It could also have been that the small Greenland-based Norse community just could not sustain the colonization attempt. Greenland itself was deserted by 1500.

The only authenticated evidence of Norse settlement in North America is at the northernmost tip of the Great Northern Peninsula. There, in a small cove, is a boat repair waystation that was discovered in 1960 by the Norwegians Helge and Anne Stine Ingstad. The present name, L'Anse aux Meadows, may come from *l'anse aux méduses*—French for "jellyfish cove." This site may have been one of the small settlements mentioned in the ancient Norse sagas, or a completely unrecorded camp. Where the main settlements were is unknown, but L'Anse aux Meadows is only a couple of day's sail north of the park, and coastal meadows suitable for typical West Norse stock farming settlements are found all along the coast of the Northern Peninsula.

The Age of Exploration

Despite reports of occasional visits by the Norse in the intervening centuries, the Italian explorer Giovanni Caboto (John Cabot) is generally credited with the rediscovery of Newfoundland—and North America—in 1497. He sailed under letters patent from King Henry VII of England, and North America was probably a bit of a disappointment since he was trying to find a route to the Orient. However, his journey prompted others to follow, and fishing vessels from France, Iberia, and England were soon making annual voyages to the inshore waters and banks around Newfoundland.

Jacques Cartier, sailing for the King of France, charted the waters around the Island in 1534, landing at St. Pauls Inlet on June 16th. This marked the beginning of European interest in the west coast, and in less than two decades an industry was founded. Basques from the Pyrenees country between France and Spain had been hunting whales in the Bay of Biscay since the 11th century. By 1500, whales were becoming scarce off the coast of Europe, and whalers were forced to venture across the North Atlantic to find more. Within fifty years Basques were whaling in the Strait of Belle Isle and the Gulf of St. Lawrence. Finding a large and profitable resource, they built the first European industrial operation in the Americas at a place that they called *Butus* or *Buytres* in southern Labrador.

According to archaeologist James Tuck, Butus (now Red Bay) became the world whaling capital between 1550 and 1600. Fifteen or more ships carrying almost a thousand men would anchor at Butus each spring, and over a fifty year period as many as ten thousand whales may have been slaughtered and processed for oil to light homes in Europe. By the 1590s whales were declining and the Basques started to take mixed cargoes of whales, seals, walrus, and cod. As catches fell and war loomed in Europe, the Basques left and were all but forgotten for 400 years. The Basque presence lives on here only in names. The west coast of Newfoundland was once called *La Côte des Basques*—the Basque Coast, and many bays and coastal features still bear their names in an altered form.

As their fishermen sailed for the New World each year to exploit the cod stocks, France and England argued over the riches of the Grand Banks, the Gulf of St. Lawrence, and the Island of Newfoundland.

Sailing Along the French Shore

France lost its claims to Newfoundland under the Treaty of Utrecht in 1713 (the same treaty that ended Basque fishing rights around the Island), but retained the right to catch and dry fish along parts of the Newfoundland coast between Cape Bonavista and Point Riche. This coast became known as the *French Shore*, and could only be used for fishing, landing, and drying cod in preparation for sailing back to France. France finally withdrew from most of her North American colonies following the loss of Québec in 1759. Britain and France settled their affairs in North America with the Treaty of Paris in 1763.

France retained two items that affected Newfoundland: the islands of St Pierre et Miquelon off the south coast of Newfoundland were kept as a base for a fishing fleet to exploit the Grand Banks, and France kept the right to fish along the shore included in the 1713 Treaty of Utrecht. Britain also agreed to disallow settlement along the Treaty Shore to prevent competition with the French fishermen. In the 1700s this Petit Nord fishery involved about 100 ships carrying 7,000 men each year.

In 1783, France and Britain signed the Treaty of Versailles (which also settled the independence of the American colonies). This treaty shifted the

French Shore westward so that it extended from Cape St. John to Cape Ray, including the coast of Gros Morne. Settlement along the shore was again declared illegal for both the French and the English, and no permanent structures could be built. Newfoundlanders were not permitted to settle along a large part of their own coast. Legalities aside, though, this did little to deter settlement.

Cook's Tours

To map the coast for treaty purposes and as an aid to safe navigation, the British Admiralty sent Captain James Cook to Newfoundland. Each summer from 1763 to 1767 he sailed to Newfoundland to work on his painstakingly accurate charts of the islands, bays, inlets, and coves. His charts also contain coastal profiles, sailing notes, hundreds of soundings, and information about the existing fishery and potential for lumbering and other development.

The Gros Morne portion of the coast was mainly surveyed in the summer of 1767. Cook was careful to gather local place names from people living and working along the shore, and it is thanks to Cook's maps that many of the early Basque and French names survived. He also named many places around the coast, including Cooks Harbour at the tip of the Great Northern Peninsula. Cook's charts opened up the previously unknown west coast of Newfoundland, and were in use unaltered until the late 1800s.

Early Settlers

Settlement of the French Shore was well underway by the end of the 1700s. There were probably people living around Bonne Bay before 1790, and certainly by the early 1800s there were several families around the bay. Joseph Bird, a merchant from Dorset in England, established a post at Woody Point around 1800 to trade in salmon, furs, cod, seal, mackerel, herring, capelin, and trout. He provided necessities such as flour, salt beef, spices, fishing supplies, building materials, snuff, combs, quilted comforters, chenille shawls, and fine calico, and a market for fish that played an important role in settling the coast. Bird & Company recruited seasonal labourers, apprentices, servants, and planters from the English counties of Dorset, Somerset, Devon, and Wiltshire. Many eventually settled around Bonne Bay and as far north as Cow Head. Other settlers came from Jersey, Scotland, France, and Canada.

Fishing was the focus of life for most settlers. At that time it was a year-round activity. Herring were caught and salted down as bait for sale to the French cod fishermen who arrived every spring. In summer the settlers caught, salted, and dried salmon that would be traded with merchants for sale to the export market. Settlement was technically forbidden, and the French could have complained about the growing outports, but it was to their advantage to have a source of bait on arrival, and they still had a relative monopoly on the cod fishery.

Families settled along the coast within rowing or sailing distance of fishing grounds. They needed clean water, a sheltered section of beach for a wharf and stage, and room for a fish storage shed and drying flakes. Each built a house and storage buildings, and tended a garden for potatoes, carrots, turnips, and cabbage. Most people kept sheep for wool and meat, but there were few cows and goats. As time went on, oxen were used for heavy farmwork and in the woods. Although some people kept ponies, they were considered to be luxuries, perhaps because few would think twice about slaughtering and eating an ox, if necessary, but most were uncomfortable with the idea of eating horse. Hunting, trapping, and fishing provided most of the food that people ate throughout the year.

In summer it was possible to travel up and down the coast by boat. Footpaths linked most communities, and in winter these were the only possible routes. Land travel was all by foot or by dog sleigh. British warships on patrol along the Treaty Shore occasionally visited and settled disputes, and other vessels carried missionaries who introduced the first semblance of an education system.

WINTERSIDE—SUMMERSIDE

Many settlers adopted a summer-winter migration pattern similar to that of the pre-European Newfoundlanders. Families lived as close as they could get to the fishing grounds in the summer, and spent their time fishing and tending vegetable gardens. At the end of the fishing season they moved

The Decker family outside their tilt at Bakers Brook, 1914.

M.S. Brainard, © J.A. Brainard

inland to sheltered wooded sites. This protected them from winter's wild gales, brought them closer to hunting and trapping grounds, and gave them a ready source of firewood to heat their small cabins.

Often these winter *tilts* were used for only one or two years, and were cold, flimsy, smoky constructions. The earliest tilts had no chimney, just a hole in the roof above an open hearth. During the winter, settlers cut timbers for boat and house building; hunted and trapped for furs and food; and made boats, floats, barrels, brooms, nets, oars, traps, and other gear. As spring approached, everyone moved back to the coast to prepare for the summer fishery. This migratory lifestyle is reflected in place names in the park: south of Woody Point is a village called Winter House Brook, and north of the town, closer to the mouth of Bonne Bay was Summerhouse (now Mudges Point or Much's Point). At Cow Head, the main summer settlement was on the peninsula surrounded by fishing grounds; today's townsite was originally called Winterside.

The winterside-summerside lifestyle continues today, in a reduced and modified way. Throughout the park and all along coast there are small summer fishing communities such as Bakers Brook, Green Point, Hickeys and Old House Rocks, where families live and work during the fishing season. Today, of course, it is easy to leave for supplies or entertainment. At the end of the season the cabins are closed up and everyone moves back to town.

Woody Point became the major commercial centre for Bonne Bay and the surrounding coast. Bird & Company was purchased by a firm from the Island of Jersey, and from 1849 to 1873 the area became known as the Jersey Room (*room* in this context meaning "mercantile establishment").

First salmon and then cod declined, then in the late 1870s herring stocks started to fail due to overexploitation. The advent of canning led the exploitation of a new species—lobster. Originally *crawlers* were considered good only for bait or as starvation food because the meat could not be preserved. Soon canning factories were established at Woody Point, Rocky Harbour, Cow Head, and St. Pauls (*factories* in the local context could mean anything from a one-family canning shed to a large merchant-owned operation). There were 33 lobster factories on the west coast by 1888, of which 4 were French.

By the 1890s most coves and inlets along the shore were occupied, including many that show no signs of habitation today. Increasing population led to disputes over the French Shore. The argument over lobster came to a boil.

France and Britain finally settled their differences in 1904, just in time for the First World War. In return for the extinguishment of her treaty rights, France accepted a cash payment and a settlement of imperial disputes in Africa in her favour. The French Shore was no more; west coast settlements were finally legitimate, and could enter the twentieth century.

After 1904 the large merchant-owned lobster canneries began to give way to smaller family-owned operations. Lobsters became less common. The herring fishery made a brief resurgence just after the turn of the century, but then

Norris Point Wharf, 1925.

failed again in 1915 and never really recovered. The resources of the sea were failing, so some people turned to trapping, fox farming, mink farming, and guiding for caribou hunters (there were no moose in the area yet) and salmon fishermen. An oil seep at Parsons Pond, known since 1812, was drilled to produce a well in 1867. By 1906 at least 26 holes had been sunk there, and a smaller number at St Pauls Inlet. Oil and gas were found, but not enough to warrant large-scale production. The wells still seep brownish paraffin-based oil at the top of the well casings. Elsewhere, the forest began to take on a greater importance.

The Rise and Fall of a Company Town

Forest along the coast had long been used for fuel and construction timber, and a few masts and spars were probably cut around Bonne Bay by the French and British. In the early 1900s lumbering became a business, changing from personal use to industrial. The great white pine and red spruce forests of eastern North America had been cut, world trade was expanding, and so was the population and the need for forest products. More wood was required for paper production and for coal mine supports. Trees were in demand.

Logging started in earnest here about seven decades after it began on the mainland, because the trees on the Island were smaller and well away from the major markets. The first records of a commercial logging operation in the park area come from around 1895 when John and Scobie McKie, brothers from Nova Scotia, built a steam-powered sawmill at Paynes Cove (later called Stanleyville). By 1901 there were nine families living there, and by 1910 the McKies employed 60 men. The St. Lawrence Timber, Pulp, and Steamship Company purchased the McKie operation in 1916, and 2 years later moved it a couple of kilometres east to Murphy's Cove where there was more land for expansion.

Stanleyville ca. 1905.

Mill manager George Simpson, a Scot, named the town Lomond, perhaps in memory of the Lomond Hills near his birthplace. His new steam-powered mill was hailed as the largest in Newfoundland. Around it rose a townsite with houses and a bunkhouse, a meal hall, a store, a school, warehouses, wharves, produce gardens, electric lights, hay fields for feeding the woods horses, and an icehouse to store food for the lumbermen. Lomond was a company town, and at its peak employed as many as 500 workers.

Although able to supply enough wood to rebuild waterfront establishments at Woody Point after a major fire in 1922, the mill did not last long. The size and volume of timber supplies had been miscalculated, and the mill cost too much to run. It closed in the early 1920s, and the Lomond operation changed from sawn timber to exporting raw pulp logs and pit props. In the 1920s and 1930s, Lomond was a model town. It had the first telephones in the park area, and was an important stopping point for large tour boats, small aeroplanes, Royal Navy vessels, and visiting dignitaries. The Island's governor general, a British prime minister, naval officers, politicians, photographers,

The lumber company town of Lomond, 1925.

geologists, and sportsmen passed through, and there was a social life that included skating, cross-country skiing, badminton, school concerts, silent movies, and a great deal of salmon fishing. The town was neatly kept, the houses all painted alike, and there were extensive flower gardens. The operation continued until 1942, when it was bought by Bowater Limited as a lumber source for its Corner Brook pulp mill.

Interested in lumber but not towns, Bowater sold Lomond's 23 houses to the residents in 1950. The town declined rapidly as the trucking of pulpwood replaced river drives and their associated employment. By 1966 there were only four families left in Lomond. The province decided that it could no longer afford to plough the road in winter, and no teacher could be found for the school. As part of the province's resettlement programme the town was all but abandoned in 1967. The town finally died when Hibbert Organ and his family left in August of the following year. Some buildings were maintained as summer cottages, and by 1972 there were 30 families summering at Lomond. In 1973 the land was expropriated by the provincial government for the establishment of Gros Morne National Park, and all of the buildings were eventually removed or demolished, except for the mill manager's home (called *St. Tecla*).

Life Around the Bay

Between the world wars, the Lomond operation and small sawmills diversified the local economy, and introduced cash to more families—the cashless fishing society was coming to an end. The first half of the 20th century was relatively prosperous, but the west coast remained the Forgotten Coast as far as the rest of Newfoundland was concerned.

A road was built between Deer Lake and Lomond in 1935, and in 1942 was extended to Woody Point. The only connection between Woody Point and the rest of the Great Northern Peninsula was by ferry in summer, and

Winter mail was delivered along the Great Northern Peninsula by dog team until 1952.

across the ice in winter. Supplies and mail were delivered to towns along the coast by schooner and coastal steamer in summer. There was still no real road northward on the Peninsula, except for a coastal path called the Mail Road.

Social Changes and Confederation

Following the war, Canada was uneasy about the American presence on the Island (the U.S. established four large air and naval bases here during the war), and England wished to divest itself of the colony. After much politicking and haranguing, Newfoundlanders were persuaded to join the Canadian confederation in 1949. Newfoundland and Labrador, the first and oldest British colony, became the last and youngest province in Canada.

Electrical power reached all of the communities in the park area between 1955 and 1967, and the technology brought with it new ideas. Catalogues, magazines, radio, and now television conveyed an idealized view of the glamour and luxury of the outside world, and transportation became easier. More and more young Newfoundlanders left for the mainland, and the population of many towns and villages declined.

Until 1952, winter mail was carried north to St. Anthony along the Mail Road by dogsled. This changed with the construction of a road up the Great Northern Peninsula after 1953. The community of Trout River remained an outport the longest. It was not until the late 1950s that a road linked it to Woody Point. The road around the north shore of Bonne Bay was completed in 1967, bypassing the ferry link from Woody Point to Norris Point. This had a drastic effect on the economic life of the south side of Bonne Bay.

Between 1954 and 1975 the provincial and federal governments attempted to centralize government and social services such as roads, telephones, electricity, water and sewer systems, health care, and education. These controversial resettlement programs uprooted 30,000 people, and left 300 abandoned communities in Newfoundland and Labrador. In the park area, Chimney Cove, Lomond, Gadds Harbour, and the summerside community on the Cow Head Peninsula were the most obvious victims of centralization schemes. People were moved into larger centres, and there was a decline in self-sufficiency in food. With less land, even fewer people raised livestock and tended gardens; modern times were changing people's relationship with the land and the sea.

THE DEVELOPMENT OF TOURISM

From the 1700s onward, vessels from France, Nova Scotia, and America stopped in Bonne Bay to resupply, as did British warships. Sportsmen came in small numbers for hunting and fishing after 1850, and one local story has the Prince of Wales arriving on a Royal Navy vessel and taking in a hunting expedition on the Long Range Mountains at the turn of the 20th century.

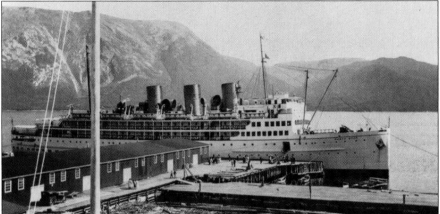

Cruise ship *North Star* at Lomond, 1930.

Naturalists and adventurers were coming to this coast as early as the 1860s. During that decade an English naturalist named William Henry Reeks lived for two years at Cow Head and wrote articles for a British zoology journal about the birds, plants, mammals, and the way of life that he experienced.

In the late 1800s the well-known Newfoundland photographer Robert Edward Holloway boated and camped along this coast. The books and prints that resulted from his visits exposed the rest of the country to the beauty of the west coast. Coastal steamers, yachts, and large cruise ships brought sightseers to the area in the 1920s. Geologists and botanists from Harvard, Yale, and other institutions around North America arrived to explore this unknown territory, and their publications encouraged others to visit.

Lee Wulff, a film maker and probably the most famous American sportsman of the period, established fly-in fishing camps at Western Brook Pond and Portland Creek in the 1940s. His films promoted this area as a destination for sightseeing and sport fishing. As roads were built it became easier to visit, and in 1959, at the suggestion of geologist Dr. David Baird, the first serious discussions were held about setting up a park in the Western Brook Pond area. After the boom-and-bust economic ride of the past, it was recognized that the establishment of a park and the tourism that it would bring could help to stabilize local economies. The beauty and significance of the landscape were keys to new opportunities.

After proposals and arguments by researchers, local spokespeople, and politicians, an agreement was reached between the provincial and federal governments. The arrangement for establishing the park required that the province resettle some of the smaller communities. So people from Lobster Cove, Bakers Brook, Green Point, Belldowns Point, and Woody Cove were enticed to move to nearby communities such as Norris Point, Rocky Harbour, and Cow Head where services could be centralized. In 1973 a federal-provincial agreement was signed for the creation of Gros Morne National Park.

Newfoundland ponies and other livestock once grazed freely throughout the area.

The establishment of the park brought national attention to the Bonne Bay area, and in 1987 the United Nations Educational, Scientific, and Cultural Organization (UNESCO) bestowed on Gros Morne the status of a World Heritage Site. Gros Morne is no longer the Forgotten Coast, and its spectacular geology, wildlife, and natural beauty continue to draw visitors from around the world and mould the lifestyle of the people who live here.

Crew of the trading schooner *Ella Frances*, about 1900.

Loggers clearing a jam on the Lomond River, 1920.

EXPLORING THE PARK'S HISTORY

There are two major history exhibits in the park: Broom Point fishing station and Lobster Cove Head lighthouse display, both of which are described in the next chapter. The park's lumber history is explored with signs at Lomond Day-use Area and the Wigwam Pond Lookoff.

View of Gros Morne and The Tickle from Woody Point.

GROS MORNE VISITOR'S GUIDE

HOW TO GET HERE

OST VISITORS ARRIVE AT THE PARK IN CARS OR charter buses, but others come on foot, by bicycle, motorbike, and boat. The closest airport is at Deer Lake, and there are car rental agencies there. Public transit is limited along this coast, but taxis and buses serve most communities. It is difficult to explore this park without transportation. Hitchhiking is usually good here in summer, but roads are often quiet and distances long. Time-saving boat crossings of Bonne Bay can be arranged with local boat owners.

To get an idea of the size of the park, remember that it takes about an hour to drive from Rocky Harbour to the northern boundary, and it is about a 90 minute drive to Trout River. Corner Brook is almost a 2 hour drive from Rocky Harbour, Deer Lake 1 hour, and St. Anthony 5 hours.

Ferry—Marine Atlantic operates the ferry service between Cape Breton and the Island of Newfoundland. For schedule information and reservations, call 1-800-341-7981.

Bus—The Viking Express bus travels along the Great Northern Peninsula, going north on three days of the week and south another three days. Also, a bus from Rocky Harbour and a van from Woody Point make the round trip to Corner Brook once a day from Monday to Friday. For schedules, call 709-634-4710.

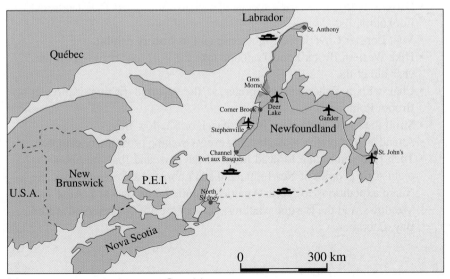

Major transportation routes to Gros Morne.

SUGGESTED ITINERARIES

Gros Morne is so large and varied that it takes time to really see it. Some suggested itineraries are outlined below.

Half a day or less—You will have to choose either the north or south tour. Stop at the roadside interpretive lookoffs to get a feeling for the scenery of the park and some of its main stories. Explore Lobster Cove Head exhibit or Broom Point, or drop in to the Visitor Centre to get information for your next visit!

One day—A day only gives you the chance to drive around and see the major scenic features of the south and north sections of the park (the Tablelands, Bonne Bay, the Long Range escarpment, etc.), or to concentrate on one intense experience from the must-do list below. You should also have time to stroll down Southeast Hills Falls Trail, Tablelands Trail, or Western Brook Beach Trail. Stop at the Visitor Centre to watch the park slide presentations and get a feel for the diversity of the park.

Two days or longer—Start at the Visitor Centre. There you can get a copy of *Tuckamore*, see the slide presentations, and get information about interpretive programs, wildlife sightings, and other points of interest. Then pick from the following list of must-do items to suit your taste:

- Drive to the south side of Bonne Bay and explore the Tablelands.
- Take the Tablelands boat tour to see a landlocked fjord and the Tablelands.
- Hike Green Gardens Trail to see the coast and meadows.
- Hike up the Lookout Trail for a view of Bonne Bay.
- If a ferry is operating across Bonne Bay, by all means take it! Watch for whales, seals, scenery, and seabirds.
- Hike Gros Morne Mountain Trail and see highlands and views.
- Drive to Norris Point for a spectacular view of the steep Tablelands and Lookout Hills.
- Visit Lobster Cove Head Lighthouse and its history exhibit.
- Hike Western Brook Pond Trail and take the boat tour between billion-year-old cliffs.
- Chat with a fisherman-interpreter at the restored fishing station at Broom Point.
- Stroll the sands at Western Brook beach or Shallow Bay.
- Attend an interpretive walk, boating events evening program, or campfire.
- Then take some time to head north of the park and find out about the prehistoric peoples of Newfoundland and Labrador at Port au Choix, the Norse expeditions to North America a millennium ago at L'Anse aux Meadows, and the Basque whaling centre of the 1500s preserved at Red Bay, Labrador.

Interpretive event, Green Point geology.   Lobster Cove Head beachwalk.

Knitting heads for lobster pots at Broom Point interpretive exhibit.

INTERPRETATION IN GROS MORNE

From late June to early September, experienced interpreters present informative guided walks, campfires, special events, and evening programs throughout the park. If you want to learn about Gros Morne's wildlife, plants, geology, or history, check bulletin boards for a list of interpretive events on land and sea, or pick up a schedule at the Visitor Centre or other park building. Regular events proceed in all weather. Fees may apply to some special events. The main interpretive facilities in the park are described below.

Visitor Reception Centre—near Rocky Harbour, with an information desk, bookstore, ticket sales area, backcountry registration service, theatres,

Marine interpretive event.

Tablelands trail interpretive walk.

Interpretive exhibit on the Gros Morne Trail.

naturalist/interpreters to answer questions, and relaxing area. Gros Morne's UNESCO World Heritage Site designation plaque is at the Centre, and a blue UNESCO flag flies alongside the Maple Leaf. The main park slide show is screened in the main theatre throughout the day, and interpretive talks are presented most evenings during the summer. Geology exhibits, caribou dioramas, interactive videos, and a photographic display highlight park themes and attractions.

Check the *Sightings Book* to find out what animals, plants, and phenomena have been noted recently.

Discovery Centre—In 2000 a large new interpretation centre opens near Woody Point. Engaging and entertaining exhibits will explore western

The Visitor Centre under a threatening sky.

Lobster Cove Head lighthouse.

Newfoundland's peculiar geological history, and show the strong effect that bedrock has had on glaciation, plant and animal distribution, and human resettlement.

Broom Point—This family fishing premises was owned and operated by the Mudge family between 1941 and 1975. In 1990 it opened to the public as an interpretive exhibit staffed by people who have lived and fished along this shore for most of their lives. These interpreters give a first-hand account of making a living from the sea.

The site consists of two original buildings: the cabin where three Mudge brothers, their wives, and children lived, and their fish store used for boats, traps, nets, and other equipment. This site has been restored to the period of the late 1960s, when Newfoundland's inshore fishery for lobster, salmon, and cod was still a major source of employment and the keystone in the

Caribou diorama at the Visitor Centre.

Western Brook Pond trailside sign.

economy. Broom Point is open daily during the summer, usually from mid-June to mid-September.

Lobster Cove Head—Perched on a headland just north of Rocky Harbour, this small lighthouse was manned by members of the Young family for three-quarters of a century. The light tower is still operated by the Canadian Coast Guard, but has been automated since the 1975.

The lightkeeper's house has been turned into a museum that tells the history of the light, and of the entire coast. This 4,500-year span of human habitation is a story of perseverance against hard weather and hard times, and of remarkable resourcefulness. Open from end of June to September.

A system of paths wends through the tuckamore forest around the lighthouse. Most of the trails lead down stairways to the beach, where you can explore tidepools for marine plants and animals. The meadows are full of wildflowers and berries, and are a great place to fly kites. Interpretive campfires are held each week in a cove below the light.

Roadside Interpretive Signs

- Western Brook Pond lookoff—how ice cut glacial troughs into the Long Range Mountains.
- Gull Rocks lookoff—East Arm fjord: why it is special, and what lives in its frigid depths.
- Burridges Gulch lookoff—how glaciers carved a hanging valley.
- Wigwam Pond lookoff—the logging history of the rich lowland forest.

On-site Exhibits or Trailside Signs

- Shallow Bay Day-use Area—signs tell the history of the Cow Head

Swimming pool at the park Recreation Complex.

peninsula, the Old Mail Road along the coast, and how fragile sand dunes and tern nesting sites are.

- Western Brook Pond Trail—signs interpret the lowland bogs, insect-eating plants of the wetlands, wildlife and wildflowers, and other features of the trail.
- Western Brook Pond shore—the ultra-pure waters of the lake, and how glaciers excavated the massive trough.
- Western Brook Beach—the fragility of the sand dunes.
- Lobster Cove Head—a map of the trail system, things to do in the area, history of the lighthouse, and how to read the signal flags.
- Gros Morne mountain Trail—an introduction to plants and animals of the arctic-alpine zone, and how to hike without disturbing them.
- Tablelands Trail parking lot—the geological formation of the Tablelands, its unusual features and how life adapted to survive there.
- Lomond Day-use Area—the rise and fall of a logging company town, illustrated with old photographs.
- Lookout Trail—a map of the route and information about plants and animals that you will see along it.
- Trout River Pond parking lot—what to do in the Trout River Pond area.

ACCESSIBLE FACILITIES

Gros Morne is attempting to make trails, buildings, and programs accessible to visitors of all abilities. This will allow everyone to experience a variety of recreational and educational experiences within the park. Facilities throughout the park have been designed to aid people with mobility problems;

Campgrounds	Berry Hill	Shallow Bay	Lomond	Trout River	Green Point
Drive-in sites	146	50	25	29	18
Walk-in sites	6	0	4	4	0
Hot Water	yes	yes	yes	yes	no
Showers	yes	yes	yes	yes	no
Flush toilets	yes	yes	yes	yes	no
Dumping Station	yes	yes	yes	no	no
Playground	yes	yes	yes	yes	no
Fireplaces	yes	yes	yes	yes	yes
Kitchen Shelters	yes	yes	yes	yes	yes

the Tablelands Boat Tour, the Visitor Centre and theatre, Lobster Cove Head Lighthouse, the Recreation Complex, the first part of the Berry Head Pond Trail, the Broom Point fish store, Shallow Bay Campground, Shallow Bay Day-use Area and beach, and all roadside lookoffs are accessible.

A heavy-duty all-terrain wheelchair is available at no charge from the Visitor Centre. It is not motorized, but can be pushed along many of the flatter park trails. Unfortunately, it does not fit easily into most car trunks. Visitors with hearing difficulties can watch close-captioned slide shows at the Visitor Centre and Lobster Cove Head Lighthouse. A telephone equipped with TDD service is available at the park Administration Building and at the Visitor Centre. Pocket-sized FM *Easy Listener* receivers are available at the Visitor Centre for use on guided walks. Please reserve 24 hours in advance by calling 709-458-2066. An interactive information kiosk at the Visitor Centre has been designed for maximum accessibility.

CAMPING AND ACCOMMODATIONS

Each of Gros Morne's five campgrounds is located in a different environment, and offers a different experience. Firewood can be bought at campgrounds or in communities. Park campsites can accommodate large recreational vehicles if they do not require water and electrical hookups. Fully serviced sites are available at two private campgrounds in the Rocky Harbour area. There are two hostels in the park area: one in Woody Point (709-453-7254, or 709-453-2470) operated by the Bonne Bay Development Association, and a private hostel in Rocky Harbour (709-458-2917).

Trout River Campground—near Trout River Day-use Area, an unsupervised freshwater beach, a boat launch, Tablelands Boat Tour, Trout River Pond Trail, and the community of Trout River. Sites are well wooded, and there are views of the Pond and the Tablelands.

Lomond Campground—near Lomond Day-use Area, boat launch and wharf, an unsupervised saltwater beach, Stanleyville Trail, and Lomond River Trail. Sites are open and grassy, or in forest. Views of Bonne Bay, Lomond River, and Killdevil Mountain. Day-use area has picnic sites, a playground, and kitchen shelters, and a solar-heated outdoor shower.

A backcountry campsite at Green Gardens.

Daniel Boisclair, GMNP

Berry Hill Campground—near Rocky Harbour, Lobster Cove Head, the park Swimming Pool, Berry Hill Pond Trail, Berry Hill Trail, and Bakers Brook Falls Trail. The Visitor Centre, six kilometres away, has evening programs throughout the summer. A separate Group Camping Area can be reserved by nonprofit and commercial groups.

Green Point Campground—between Sally's Cove and Rocky Harbour; on the coast, partly in old field and partly in tuckamore. A section of the Old Mail Road Trail starts here, there is good cobble beach to walk on, and the summer fishing community of Green Point is just across the cove. This campground is kept open for winter camping, but there is no running water available then.

Shallow Bay Campground—near Cow Head, the Shallow Bay Trail, Shallow Bay Day-use Area, and an unsupervised saltwater beach with four kilometres of sand and grass-covered dunes. The sites are grassy and sheltered. There is a small outdoor theatre for evening programs.

Backcountry Camping

Wilderness camping is available along several of the longer trails in the park. Designated campsites have only minimal facilities, usually wooden tent pads (to reduce trampling of the soil and to keep your tent off the wet ground), a food locker or bear pole (for storing food so that it does not attract bears), and a pit privy. The showers at these sites are cold and only occur on overcast days. Read the following trail descriptions for details about the campsites. A reservation system ensures that sites are not over-booked or overused, and you can register at the Visitor Centre and most other park facilities.

Roofed Accommodations

Hotels, motels, Bed & Breakfasts, cabins, and hostels operate in communities throughout the park, There is information in *Tuckamore*, or you can consult a copy of the *Newfoundland and Labrador Travel Guide* for rates, descriptions, and phone numbers. For Provincial tourist information, write to: Department of Tourism, Culture, and Recreation, P.O. Box 8730, St. John's, Nfld., A1B 4K2, Tel: 1-800-563-6353, Fax: 709-729-1965.

INFORMATION ABOUT THE PARK

Tuckamore—This is Gros Morne's annual newspaper, and the users' guide to the park. It contains maps, trail descriptions, articles about wildlife and new facilities, listings of community services, and other useful information about the park. Available at the park gate and Visitor Centre, or you can send for a free copy.

Gros Morne National Park home page—Up-to-date information about Gros Morne can be found at www.grosmorne.pch.gc.ca and parkscanada.pch.gc.ca will call up the Parks Canada website.

Rocks Adrift—An award-winning 56-page soft-cover book about the geology of the park. Illustrated with colour photographs and drawings, it describes the geological evolution of the park area from 1.25 billion years ago to the beginning of the last Ice Age, and interprets major geological attractions that can be reached by road and trail.

Geology, Topography, and Vegetation, Gros Morne National Park—An atlas of the park. Published by the Geological Survey of Canada, this sheet of four colourful 1:150,000-scale maps, site sketches, and interpretive notes tells the story of the park's bedrock geology, glacial geology, topography, and vegetation, and the complex ways in which they interact.

Gros Morne National Park Trail Guide—This 1:100,000-scale colour map of the park is printed on waterproof, tearproof paper, with trail profile drawings and trail descriptions on the back.

When Continents Collide—An award-winning slide presentation, shown at the Visitor Centre theatre, that explains the fascinating geological evolution of the park. The park area has been important in understanding the concept of plate tectonics, and the park's UNESCO World Heritage Site designation is based on its geological significance; 11 minutes long.

A Wonderful Fine Coast—Another award-winning slide presentation at the

Visitor Centre. It is an introduction to Gros Morne; 17 minutes long. Both shows are contained on a video available at the Co-operating Association bookstore.

Interactive Video Kiosks—These kiosks at the Visitor Centre show video clips of each of the park trails, campgrounds, and other facilities.

Hiking the Long Range—This 15 minute video is required viewing for anyone registering to backpack in the Long Range.

For more information—Gros Morne National Park, P.O. Box 130, Rocky Harbour, Nfld., A0K 4N0, Canada. Tel: 709-458-2066, Fax: 709-458-2059.

RECREATION

Kite Flying—Breezes are dependable, and it is more common for there to be too much wind than too little. The best places for flying are the meadows at Lobster Cove Head and St. Pauls marsh, and Western Brook and Shallow Bay beaches.

Western Brook Pond boat tour.   Trout River Pond boat tour.

Swimming—The Gros Morne Recreation Complex is an airy cedar-beam building overlooking Rocky Harbour. It operates during the summer, and contains a 25-metre pool, a children's wading pool, and a large hot whirlpool. The pool schedule includes general swims, family swims, swimming classes, and various water safety and training programs.

Unsupervised outdoor swimming is best in the sheltered beaches at Shallow Bay, Lomond, and Trout River Pond. There is lots of plant and animal life to see with a mask and snorkel at the ocean beaches. River pools are great for cooling off, but beware of fast currents and hidden rocks.

Rock Climbing, Mountain Biking, Scuba Diving—Visitors interested in these activities in the park area are encouraged to speak to park staff for information about local hazards and regulations.

Boat Tours—*Tablelands Boat Tour*: Trout River Pond and the Tablelands have some of the most overwhelming scenery in the park. The boat tour leaves from the day-use area. No hike is required to get to the boat, and both site and boat are accessible for people with mobility impairments. An interpretive tape explains the Tablelands' geological history and other features of this landlocked fjord during the 30-kilometre, 2.5 hour tour. Bring a windbreaker.

Western Brook Pond Boat Tour: This great lake is another landlocked fjord, with massive cliffs and veil-like waterfalls. The walk in to the lake shore (where the boat tour leaves) usually takes 40 minutes. There are interpretive signs along the trail and an exhibit at the waiting area. The boat cruises through what may be the purest fresh water in the world, taking 2.5 hours to cover the 30-kilometre round trip through the park's best known scenic feature. Bring a windbreaker.

Private boat tours: Several operate in the park area. Check *Tuckamore* and the Visitor Centre for more information about tours on Bonne Bay, St. Pauls Inlet, and elsewhere.

Watercraft—Park boat launches are located at the Trout River Pond, Lomond, and Mill Brook day-use areas. Public launches are at Woody Point, Norris Point, Rocky Harbour, St. Pauls, and Cow Head. There are government wharves at most coastal communities, and park wharves at Trout River (used by the tour boat), Lomond, and Mill Brook.

- *Motorized boats:* Power boats can be used on Trout River Pond, Bonne Bay, and St. Pauls Inlet. For more information contact the Visitor Centre.
- *Sailboats*: The deep arms of Bonne Bay are accessible to sailing vessels.
- *Canoes and River Kayaks:* It can be dangerous to use an open boat on St. Pauls Inlet and Western Brook Pond because sudden winds raise high waves and the shoreline includes long sections of cliff with no landing sites. Streams are small and bouldery, with waterfalls and shallow rapids and insufficient water flow for boating.
- *Sea Kayaks:* Experienced sea kayakers should have few problems in Bonne Bay. Mornings and evenings are often calm, but strong winds usually arise at midday. The park's outer coast is unsheltered and can be

dangerous because of unpredictable weather conditions and large swells. If you wish to try sea kayaking, introductory paddles, day trips, and interpretive tours are offered by outfitters in the park area. See *Tuckamore* for information.

DRESSING FOR THE WEATHER

For outdoor activities in either summer or winter you should have clothes that are warm and windproof: always carry a fleece or sweater and a windbreaker. Raingear (jacket and pants) rarely go unused if you are here for several days. Footwear should be waterproof or fast drying. Sneakers and other strong light footwear will be comfortable on most of the short and level trails in the park. For longer trails, sturdier hiking shoes or hiking boots are recommended. Gaiters are very useful in the backcountry for travel through snow, for hiking through mucky terrain, and for fast brook crossings. They will also protect your calves from scratches when beating through tuckamore. Hiking sandals are great for river crossings and the muddiest wades, and useful as camp wear to give your feet a rest from hiking boots.

If you plan a trip onto the hills, even Gros Morne mountain, remember that it will be cooler up there than on the lowland, and that the winds can be 2 to 2.5 times stronger. Don't forget sunscreen and sunglasses. Carry a daypack for extra clothing, and bring at least a litre of drinking water per person. In spring and fall, gloves and a hat are a good idea, for both highlands and windswept shore. The gloves may also come in handy on rough steep terrain. A collapsible ski pole or hiking staff will reduce the strain on your knees during long descents over uneven ground. Two last words of advice: insect repellent.

BITING INSECTS

Frequent breezes and winds mean that biting flies are rarely a problem along the coast or on the highlands. Inland, however, they get serious. The park has mosquitoes and blackflies in July and August, occasional clouds of no-see-ems (or sandflies), and deerflies (locally called *stouts*) lurk in bushes. It is worth carrying a strong insect repellent for when you crack and decide that you have to use it. Repellent is usually necessary only three or four times during the summer for any hiker hardened to flies.

DRINKING WATER

Although much of the water in the park is stained brown by percolation through organic soils, it is drinkable. Giardiasis (beaver fever) has been reported from communities nearby, and could be transported to any waterbody in the park by an infected human. For safety's sake, the park recommends that all water from streams, ponds, and springs be boiled or filtered before drinking.

ANIMALS AND PLANTS

Please treat all wild animals with respect. Bears, moose, and caribou are much larger than you, and have the potential to do a lot of damage. Do not approach or harass wildlife, large or small. It is unlawful to feed animals in a national park, and when animals get too used to humans and human food, they may have to be destroyed. Ask for a pamphlet about bear safety when you enter the park.

There is no poison ivy in Gros Morne, and there are no poisonous snakes. Bees and wasps tend to be docile unless annoyed. Ants may nip, but they do not sting. Some of the larger jellyfish have stings, and should be avoided. As elsewhere, various roots, stems, mushrooms, and berries are poisonous, but you should not be consuming the park in any case.

PETS IN THE PARK

Pets are allowed on most hiking trails in Gros Morne National Park. They must be kept on a leash at all times (verbal control is *not* sufficient). Pets are not allowed on Gros Morne Mountain Trail or on the Western Brook Pond Boat Tour (a terminus for both highland traverses), or on groomed ski trails. Pet-sitting services may be available—ask at the Visitor Centre. The closest veterinary clinic is in Corner Brook.

FISHING

A provincial inland fishing license is required for nonresidents to fish in Gros Morne. Retail outlets such as service stations, hardware stores, etc. sell licenses. A salmon license is required on scheduled waters. For seasons and limits consult the *Anglers' Guide*. Trout River, Lomond River, East Branch Lomond River, and Deer Arm Brook are scheduled rivers and restricted to fly-fishing. Western Brook and its tributaries are closed to fishing. Amendments to these regulations will be in effect when Gros Morne is finally proclaimed under the National Parks Act.

Fly-fishing has a long history in the park area. An article by the 19th century naturalist Henry Reeks contains the earliest record (probably around Cow Head): "In September, 1866, I watched two young men fishing for trout with the most wretched specimens of home-made 'flies' I ever saw, being composed of a small gull's feather and a piece of red woolen lining from an old coat." Speckled trout were common in the brooks, and runs of large silvery sea trout and Atlantic salmon swarmed up rivers each summer. Despite Reeks' disdain for the men's flies, "They captured seventy-five trout in less than two hours," somewhat exceeding current catch limits.

For those who would rather watch fish than worry them, with a mask and snorkel you can observe salmon and trout in many brooks without disturbing them. Salmon leap up the Lomond River Falls, just a short walk from Lomond River Lodge on Highway 431. Another place to watch them is Big Falls at Sir Richard Squires Provincial Park, south of Gros Morne.

COMMUNITY SERVICES

For a current listing of the services available in communities in the park area, consult the *Newfoundland and Labrador Travel Guide*, and the park newspaper *Tuckamore*.

Availability of supplies—Some camping supplies are available in the park area, and basic supplies can be obtained from stores in the communities. Naphtha (white gas), kerosene, and propane are readily available.

Health and hospitals—There is a hospital at Norris Point (709-458-2201), and doctors are on duty in clinics at Trout River, Woody Point, and Cow Head for part of the week. The only pharmacy and dentist in the park area are in Norris Point.

Post Offices—Mail can be sent and received in Cow Head, St. Pauls, Rocky Harbour, Norris Point, Birchy Head, Woody Point, and Trout River.

Police—There is a Royal Canadian Mounted Police station in Rocky Harbour. Phone 709-458-2222.

Park Wardens—The park operates warden stations at Birchy

© Michael Burzynski

Baker's Brook Falls Trail.

Snowshoeing with grey jays.

Backcountry skiing near Eastern Arm Pond.

Badweather Pond.

Head (709-453-7223), Rocky Harbour (709-458-2816), and Cow Head (709-243-7260).
Banks—The only bank and bank machine in the park area are in Rocky Harbour. The next closest is at Deer Lake.

WINTER ACTIVITIES

Throughout the winter, the Visitor Centre near Rocky Harbour is open during business hours. Some accommodations and restaurants remain open in the communities to provide for winter users, check with the park Visitor Centre for information. Winter camping is available at Green Point Campground, where there is an enclosed kitchen building with a wood stove.

Cross-country (Nordic) Skiing

The park has a well developed cross-country ski system, with 50 kilometres of groomed trails. Off-trail skiing opportunities are almost unlimited. Ski season extends from mid-January to early April. Weather conditions change rapidly. Windchill can lower the effective temperature during high winds, and blowing snow reduces visibility. Because of this, groomed trails run as much as possible in forest, avoiding open bogs. Be sure to take extra warm clothing, and sunglasses and sunscreen for glare. Dogs are not allowed on groomed trails.

For more information about trails, safety, and conditions, see the *Cross-country Skiing* brochure. During winter, call the park *Ski Line*

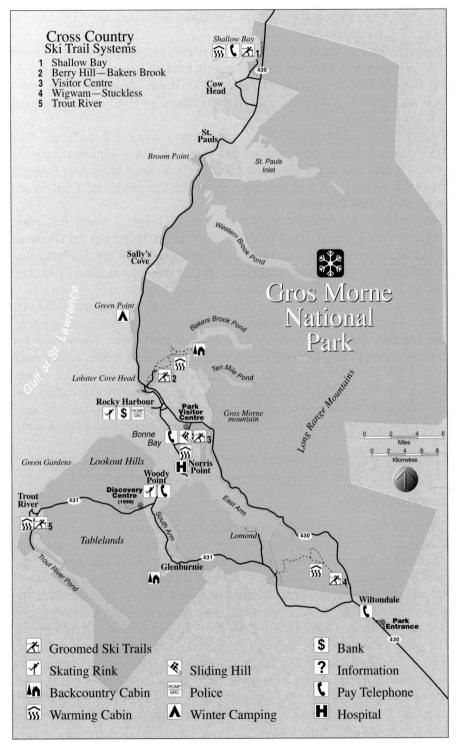

Cross Country
Ski Trail Systems

1 Shallow Bay
2 Berry Hill—Bakers Brook
3 Visitor Centre
4 Wigwam—Stuckless
5 Trout River

Shallow Bay

430

Cow
Head

St.
Pauls

Broom Point

St. Pauls
Inlet

Western Brook Pond

Sally's
Cove

Gros Morne
National
Park

Gulf of St. Lawrence

Green Point

Bakers Brook Pond

Lobster Cove Head

Ten Mile Pond

Rocky Harbour

RCMP
GRC

Park
Visitor
Centre

Gros Morne
mountain

Long Range Mountains

Bonne
Bay

0   2   4   6
Miles

0   2   4   6   8
Kilometres

Green Gardens

Lookout Hills

Norris
Point

Woody
Point

Trout
River

431

Discovery
Centre
(1999)

East Arm

South Arm

Tablelands

Lomond

430

Trout River Pond

Glenburnie

431

Wiltondale

Park
Entrance

430

🎿 Groomed Ski Trails		💲 Bank
🛼 Skating Rink	🛷 Sliding Hill	❓ Information
🏚 Backcountry Cabin	RCMP GRC Police	📞 Pay Telephone
♨ Warming Cabin	Λ Winter Camping	H Hospital

Winter facilities in Gros Morne National Park.

for updates on trail conditions: 709-458-2066. Following are brief descriptions of groomed ski trails.

Wigwam Pond to Stuckless Pond—16.5 kilometres one way, with one loop; rolling terrain with a few small hills, mostly through forest. There is a warming cabin 4.5 kilometres from Highway 430. If you intend to do the entire trail, it is good to have a second car at the Stuckless Pond end or you must retrace your tracks.

Berry Hill to Bakers Brook—18.5 kilometres return, in three loops. This trail passes through open bogland and forest, and is a relatively easy ski over flat land and small hills. There are two warming cabins, one 2 km in from the parking lot, and the other about 6.5 kilometres in. Caribou are often seen along this trail.

Shallow Bay—6.8 kilometres of trail in three loops, a short, flat, easy, beginners' trail near the community of Cow Head. It follows the Old Mail Road along the back of the dunes—the route used until the 1950s by dog teams carrying mail. Dense tuckamore shields skiers from wind. A kitchen shelter at the campground is enclosed as a warming hut.

Visitor Centre Ski Trails—seven trails of different lengths and difficulty, with a total length of 11 kilometres. The four south of the Centre are double tracked, for classic skiing. One loop to the north is groomed for freestyle skiing, another loop is lit for night use. There is also a snow park with a hill groomed for sliding, tubing, snowboarding and novice downhill skiers. The nearby Visitor Centre offers cross-country ski rentals, and contains a ski waxing room and a comfortable warm-up lounge with fireplace. Passes for use of the ski trails are available here and in park communities.

Trout River—three loops through forest with a total length of 5 kilometres. A kitchen shelter at the day-use area is enclosed as a warming hut.

Backcountry Skiing

There are many superb backcountry ski routes in the park. These range from a couple of hours to a day or more in duration. The Co-operating Association operates two backcountry cabins that skiers can rent as base camps for longer trips. These two-storey cabins are equipped with wood stoves, gas lights and ranges, and indoor toilets. Do not underestimate the dangers of off-trail skiing. Ice bridges, lake crossings, steep descents and ascents, avalanche conditions, and the possibility of getting lost are some of the natural hazards that you will encounter. You must be prepared with appropriate and dependable equipment, food, drink, warm clothing, and emergency supplies. Skis can quickly carry you a long way from the road, hypothermia can attack fast, and night falls early in winter—it gets dark around 5:30 in the afternoon in February. For information about routes and hazards, ask at the Visitor Centre.

Snowshoeing

Any trail, in fact almost anywhere in the park, is a good place to snowshoe. Small and inexpensive bearpaw-style snowshoes are available in many local shops. Although slower than skiing, snowshoes are easier to manage in dense forest or alders.

WALKING & HIKING TRAILS

Gros Morne is a park for hikers. Its diverse habitats and scenery provide a constantly changing panorama for anyone who takes the time to explore. The park's 90 kilometres of trails range from short, level, and easy to long, steep, and extremely strenuous. Some trails can be walked in minutes, others are definitely hikes, and take many hours. All are built and maintained to standards, and only brief sections of some of the longest are reserved for masochists. If you stay on the established trails when hiking, it will help to minimize damage to vegetation and soils. Please pack out all of your garbage, and recycle or dispose of it responsibly.

Hikers wishing to stay at backcountry campsites or to hike the two traverses must register and purchase a permit at the park Visitor Centre. Campfires are allowed in fire pits at park campgrounds, but are prohibited along trails, hiking routes, and at noncoastal campsites.

Please read the following descriptions carefully or watch the interactive programs at the Visitor Centre to see whether a particular trail is suited to your hiking inter-

View of Western Brook dunes from Steve's Trail.

Shallow Bay beach.

Western Brook Pond Trail.

Western Brook Beach Trail.

Snug Harbour Trail.

Green Point Trail.

ests, and whether your body is suited to the trail! For a detailed map, trail profiles, and more information, see the park *Trail Guide*.

Community trails at Cow Head, Norris Point, and Trout River lead to scenic viewpoints; enquire locally for information.

Shallow Bay Trail—4-kilometre return trail that starts at Shallow Bay Day-use Area. Until the 1970s, the Day-use Area was the site of a community called Belldowns Point, and a graveyard lies hidden in trees to the south. This level coastal trail follows the Old Mail Road through a dense fringe of wind-dwarfed tuckamore forest, past old clearings, into Shallow Bay Campground, then north along the back of sand dunes to Slants River, where it ends. This was the only overland route up the Great Northern Peninsula until the mid 1960s. A boardwalk crosses the dunes to the beach, and makes an interesting return loop to the Day-use Area. This trail is a pleasant sunset stroll if you are staying at the campground, and takes about an hour.

Steve's Trail—1-kilometre return trail at Broom Point, leading to one of the park's most beautiful panoramas. The trail takes a winding route through tuckamore, past sandy Graveyard Cove to a coastal meadow on the north shore of Western Brook. From the meadow there is a superb view of the dark portals of Western Brook gorge. In the foreground, a long sandbar curves away from dunes that define the mouth of Western Brook.

Western Brook Beach Trail—half-kilometre return trail through tuck-

Lobster Cove Head.

amore forest to a long sandy beach. Do not swim in the ocean here, there is a strong undertow.

Western Brook Pond Trail—7-kilometre return trail. Although this is the most heavily used of the park trails, it is still possible to have it all to yourself early in the day, in the evening, or out of season. This trail begins at a large parking lot. The direct route to the Pond is a 3 kilometre walk that takes 40 minutes from the parking lot.

The trail crosses bogs and low limestone ridges to the shore of the Pond. About 2 kilometres in, the trail splits. The direct route to the Pond lies straight ahead, and to the left is a scenic route that is one kilometre longer. Both portions of the trail end up at the boat tour dock, so this loop can be walked in either direction.

At the shore of the Pond is a small waiting building and a deck with an interpretive exhibit about this deep pristine lake and models that show what the area looked like during glaciation.

Snug Harbour Trail—9 kilometres return, a northern spur off the Western Brook Pond Trail, and starts at a small bridge across the brook. This seasonal bridge is usually in place from mid-June to mid-October, water level permitting. If you want to hike this trail out of season you will have to wade the brook. Beware of the sharp bridge bolts. From the bridge, the trail winds through forest and across a pebble beach to reach the primitive campsite at the foot of the hills. There are four tent sites at Snug Harbour.

Beyond the campsite, a rough trail heads uphill and onto the plateau. This is the start of the North Rim Traverse. This undeveloped trail is very steep, and the boggy soil is often muddy because of heavy moose traffic. To experience a part of the plateau, you can camp at Snug Harbour and make a day trip to the top. From the cliff tops there are amazing views of the Pond below. Read the North Rim Traverse description before hiking on

Bakers Brook Falls, as seen from the trail lookoff.

the plateau—there is no trail on top. Do not attempt any highland hike in low cloud or without a map and compass.

Stag Brook Trail—9-kilometre return trail, a southern spur off Western Brook Pond Trail. It follows the shore of the pond through forest and bog to a quiet beach. There are great views of the gorge and the escarpment of the Long Range. Boggy sections of the trail are protected with boardwalk.

Green Point Trail—6-kilometre return trail. Start from Green Point Campground or from the parking lot on the northern bank of Bakers Brook. The trail follows the Old Mail Road, hugging the upper beach and then cutting through the shelter of the tuckamore. Watch for migrating ducks and shorebirds in the marshy ponds and coastal wetlands. Large cobbles and the tangle of driftwood indicate that this section of coast is frequently hammered by heavy seas.

Berry Head Pond Trail—2-kilometre loop around the pond, with several lakeside lookoff platforms. The first half kilometre is wheelchair accessible. The rest is fairly level with boardwalk to protect wetlands and to keep walkers dry. The trail follows the lakeside through a forest of contorted trees that have been crushed by the weight of wind-drifted snow. After the forest, the trail runs out onto a bog dotted with wild rose, irises, pitcherplants, Canada burnet, and various bog shrubs.

Lobster Cove Head Trails—2-kilometre loop. The lighthouse is part of an interpretive exhibit/museum that tells the long history of the coast. Around the lighthouse is a system of short trails leading to lookoff points, old fields, through the tuckamore forest, and down staircases to the beach. A map at the parking lot shows the trails.

This meadow is a great place for families to walk, fly kites, or picnic. On the beach are cliffs of crumpled limestone and shale, and pools filled with marine life. The seaweeds are very slippery, especially after a rain, and the base of the cliffs can be dangerous because rock is always crumbling loose from above. If you handle tidepool organisms, please replace them quickly, or they will die.

Bakers Brook Falls—10-kilometre return trail, 2 to 3 hours. This trail leaves from a parking lot in Berry Hill Campground. The trail passes through a fen rich with wild orchids and other wildflowers, then enters boreal forest, passes a beaver pond, crosses bogs and then leads into a regenerating stand of balsam fir killed by hemlock looper. When the trail reaches the river it turns downstream to a viewpoint over the wide step-like falls.

Berry Hill Trail—1.5-kilometre return trail. This is a Gros Morne mountain hike scaled down for small children! The trail rises from the parking lot in Berry Hill Campground, up the small prominent hill over staircases, to the top where it makes a loop, and then descends the same way. From lookoffs at the top there are good views of the campground, the sea, the coastal lowlands, and the Long Range escarpment rising in the distance.

Gros Morne Trail, climbing the gully.   View of Ten Mile Pond from Gros Morne.

© Michael Burzynski

Daniel Boisclair, GMNP

Southeast Brook Falls.

Watch for wave-smoothed rocks near the summit that date back to 12,000 years ago when sea level was higher and this hill was a small island.

Berry Hill Pond Trail—2-kilometre level loop trail. It can be reached from the Group Camping Area in Berry Hill Campground and from the three camping loops. Watch for animals in the pond, and wildflowers in the forest. Beavers have cut trees, built lodges, and dug canals all around the pond. One section of the trail passes through a stand of balsam fir killed by hemlock looper. It is now regenerating in small trees, ferns, and raspberry bushes.

Gros Morne Trail (James Callaghan Trail)—16-kilometre round trip, a long difficult hike that usually takes 6 to 8 hours. Read the trail brochure, available at the Visitor Centre, before you go. The trail starts as a gradual 310-metre rise through forest and open heath with rest benches and an outhouse about half way to the mountain, then through forest again until the trees become more wind stunted, then give way to heath and wetlands at the foot of the mountain. A resting area and exhibit overlook the gully that leads hikers up the mountain, and for anyone not hiking the whole trail, this makes a good turn-around point.

From the exhibit the trail winds to the mountain, where it splits to form a loop. The left-hand section heads up the steep gully to the top of the mountain. This is the most difficult part of the trail—a 500-metre climb over quartzite blocks. Near the top of the gully, to the left, the going gets steeper,

Photographing orchids, Lomond River Trail.

© Michael Burzynski

until a clamber over the rim ends on top of the second highest mountain on the Island.

Wildlife on top includes woodland caribou, rock ptarmigan, willow ptarmigan, Arctic hares, and horned larks. Please do not approach the animals, and do not build cairns or otherwise disturb the rocks and vegetation of the mountaintop.

Please do not leave the trail; you will damage the mountain soils, and might harass the wildlife. Cairns mark the trail in case of low cloud. At the northern edge of the mountain there is a superb view of Ten Mile Pond. The trail begins to descend through tuckamore, and curves around to a pond in Ferry Gulch. The backcountry campsite there has three pads. Winds can be very strong, so tents should be tied down securely. The descent continues across scree to the base of the mountain. If you have knee problems, a collapsible cross-country ski pole or a hiking staff will be of some help here. Dogs and fires are not allowed. This

Barrett & McKay, GMNP

Lookout Trail, near the summit.

Green Gardens coastline.

trail is closed until July because of late snow, wet soils, and animals raising young.

This hike is not appropriate for small children. Prepare yourself before trying this trail, and hike only in good weather. It can be very cold and windy on top. There is no water on top, so bring a sufficient supply (soft drinks will only make you thirstier). Wear strong footwear with a thick sole, or you will bruise your feet. Bring a windbreaker or raingear, and do not forget a lunch, sunglasses, and sunscreen. Do not begin this long hike late in the day, or you might walk out in the dark.

Southeast Brook Falls Trail—1-kilometre return walk through woods to the top of the falls. A fenced viewpoint overlooks the plummeting water. These falls are most impressive in the spring and after a heavy rain, when the mist that they raise looks like smoke billowing from the forest.

Lomond River Trail—6-kilometre one-way trail that is best hiked with cars left at both ends. From the parking

Interpretive exhibit, Tablelands Trail.

lot on Highway 431 a boardwalk trail leads across a rich fen with lady's-slipper orchids and other wildflowers. Please help us protect them. Two branch trails lead to the right: the first is the start of Stuckless Pond Trail, and the second is a fishing spur leading to the Lomond River.

Lomond River Trail continues to the left, through forested fen, and then into a mixed woodland that is the most diverse forest in the park. It contains trees such as black ash, red maple, and white pine, all of which reach their northern limit at Bonne Bay. Forest flowers include round-leaved orchid, spotted coral-root, and one-leaved rein-orchis. There are a few small hills along the way, and the trail is open and well defined. The trail crosses several small brooks, and you will pass signs of logging throughout the forest. Near the end of the trail, a large slab pile spills into a quiet pond—

The terminus of Trout River Pond Trail.

the remains of a small push mill. The trail ends at the road beside the fields of Killdevil Camp.

Stuckless Pond Trail—9.5-kilometre return trail, 3 to 4 hours. The start of this trail is the same as the Lomond River Trail. Turn right at the first junction, and continue through the forest to an old woods road. There the trail turns left, and heads down to the Lomond River where it crosses a suspension bridge, then rises uphill. At the top of the hill the trail splits and circumnavigates Stuckless Pond.

Loggers cut around this pond in the mid-1930s. Stumps, logging roads, camp clearings, and other signs of their work are evident everywhere, including a dam at the outlet to the lake. This is a good trail for autumn hikes and wildlife.

Stanleyville Trail—4-kilometre return trail, 2 to 3 hours. It leads to the turn-of-the-century lumber town of Stanleyville. The trail is a climb through mixed forest and past signs of logging. Stumps are all that remain of the large white pines that once grew here. A few scraggly small pines survive on the ridge tops. Near Stanleyville a modern-day domestic harvest block is on the left of the trail. From there the trail descends to the terraced townsite.

The Long Range Traverse.

The only remains of the town and mill are part of a steam engine, meadows, and cultivated plants such as damson plums, musk mallow, queen of the meadow, and monkshood that have survived untended for 75 years. Three back-country campsites are spread along the beach, but there are no tent pads. You may have a campfire here, but please use the hearths provided, and burn only driftwood or provided wood. Do not take branches or trunks from the forest.

Return the same way, or hike back along the coast if the tide is low. Be careful, some sections are slippery and a short climb is necessary at one point.

Lookout Trail—5-kilometre return hike (2.5 hours) that offers a chance to see the highlands and the views without the difficulty of hiking Gros Morne. It is a steady climb through the forest, past the treeline, and out onto the boggy top of the plateau. There boardwalk protects wetlands from hikers, and makes it possible to walk comfortably. Watch for forest orchids, insect-eating plants, ptarmigan and moose. The midpoint of the trail is a platform on Partridgeberry Hill with the best panoramic view in the park: Bonne Bay, the Tickle, Gros Morne, the Long Range, the Lookout Hills, and the Tablelands. From there the trail loops back downhill.

Green Gardens Trail—Two different parking lots mark the entrances to this trail system. Most hikers start from the westernmost (Long Pond) entrance. From there it is a 9-kilometre hike (3 to 4 hours) to the shore and back on the same trail, or a more

Ponds, bogs, and rock knobs dot the highlands.

The top of the gully at the back of Western Brook Pond.

ambitious 16-kilometre round trip (6 to 8 hours) to the coast, along the meadows to Wallace Brook then back to the parking lot along a loop trail. Two river fords must be waded along the latter route.

The first part of the trail crosses peridotite barrens, then descends to the shore through forest. At the coast, the trail enters a series of meadows that stretches towards Wallace Brook. Three tent pads are provided in the first meadow. Fires are permitted on the beach, but *not* in the meadows or at the pads. Below the campsites, stairs descend to a beach of dark volcanic sand, a sea cave and wide marine platform to the north, and a small brook with several waterfalls to the south. Sea stacks line this section of coast. Keep an eye on the tides if you are walking along the beach. A second campsite has four pads, and is near the northeastern end of the meadows. From there, a trail leads up a very steep forested hill and down the other side to the mouth of Wallace Brook, where a campsite with two pads is located.

The trail then fords the brook (there is no bridge), and heads south. It splits at another ford: cross the brook to return to the Long Pond parking lot, or continue alongside the brook to reach the Wallace Brook parking lot.

Tablelands Trail—4-kilometre return trail (2 hours) along an old roadbed. It passes typical wildflowers, stunted trees, and geological features of the Tablelands area, and ends at the side of Winter House Brook offering a panorama of the Tablelands, a deep cirque valley, and Trout River Gulch. Watch for insect-eating plants, patterned ground, and snakeskin-patterned serpentinized rock. Travertine has cemented parts of the brook's bank.

Trout River Pond Trail—14-kilometre return trail (4 to 5 hours) parallels the north shore of Trout River Small Pond. The first few kilometres pass through shaded boreal forest. Then the vegetation dwindles to larch scrub and serpentine barrens. The trail crosses rocky barrens at the base of the Tablelands plateau, with huge alluvial fans, debris chutes, patterned ground, arctic-alpine plants, and travertine seeps. The trail provides views of the Narrows between the two ponds, and a peep into the Big Pond.

MAP AND COMPASS ROUTES

The wilderness of the Long Range Mountains is the ultimate hiking challenge that Gros Morne National Park has to offer. The scenery, wildlife, and solitude are unmatched in Eastern Canada. *There are no marked trails and you must rely entirely on map and compass navigation to complete these traverses.*

Pre-trip orientation is essential. The park has a scheduled briefing service with an experienced backcountry attendant at the Visitor Centre. Before you can register and receive a backcountry permit you must watch the video *Hiking in the Long Range*. It contains advice to prepare you for your hike.

Hikers get lost on the highlands almost every year. In 1995 the park began to make wilderness transmitters available, for a small rental fee. Wardens monitor backcountry permit returns. Should a search be necessary, the transmitter can be used to locate you quickly and relatively inexpensively.

Because of late snowmelt on the highlands, the route is not usually open until July. Towards the end of September there will be freezing temperatures at night, and by late October a chance of snow. For both routes, hikers must walk to the shore of Western Brook Pond and take the boat to the back of the Pond. Be sure to make a reservation! Only registered hiking groups are allowed to disembark.

Limestone arches, Cow Head.

Tide pools, Cow Head.

Long Range Traverse—Although this traverse is only 35-kilometres as the crow flies between Western Brook Pond and Gros Morne mountain, you should budget four to five days to hike it comfortably. Fog due to low cloud often makes navigation impossible.

The first leg is a 4 hour climb up the back of the gorge to the plateau top an elevation gain of about 530-metres with a superb view. The Long Range plateau itself is a mix of glacially smoothed rock ridges, forested valleys, shallow ponds, and peaty wetlands. There are 3 primitive campsites located about 6 hours apart. Moose and caribou are abundant, and their trails lead in all directions. Remember, they are not necessarily going your way!

Hiking on the highlands is anything but flat, and the route is a continuous series of hills and valleys, with detours around ponds and tuckamore. There is really no way to keep your feet dry on this trek, so bring light footwear for camp use—your feet will thank you. Be prepared for flies in July and August. Difficult sections of the route will be pointed out when you register, so keep these in mind as you hike—these are the places that hikers are most likely to go astray.

The best views along the traverse are at the begining and the end. Western Brook gorge and Ten Mile Pond gorge are spectacular. If you have the time and energy, take a side trip to see the back of Bakers Brook gorge too.

The trail descends opposite a small pond on Crow Cliff, and you can look straight down on the Ferry Gulch primitive campsite. The descent into Ferry Gulch is muddy, slippery, and steep. Take your time!

North Rim Traverse—Another unmarked route, this 27-kilometre traverse usually takes 2 to 3 days. Although shorter than the Long Range Traverse, this hike is in some ways more difficult. As with the Long Range hike, you ascend the back of the gorge. Climbing out of the rocky bowl, you head north by compass bearing, and then turn west to parallel the north rim of the

Kayakers at Shag Cliff, near Burnt Hill Trail.

Waterfall and pool, Glenburnie.

Playing on the sand flats, Shallow Bay.

Watching wildlife along Highway 430.

Trout River fishing boats, near the Old Man Trail.

Sally's Cove.

Exploring Woody Point on foot.

Pond. The terrain is very difficult, with lakes and long stretches of dense tuckamore to negotiate. The recommended campsite is on the shore of Long Pond. The last part of the traverse covers relatively open barrens. It is worth taking a side trip to the rim of the Pond. From the edge of the cliff you look down 600-metres to the black water below, and to the broad coastal lowlands stretching to the sea.

The descent starts beside a deep gully with a waterfall cascading into it. A large boulder topped with a rock cairn marks the beginning of a primitive trail, which winds down through windswept heathland, into low tuckamore near the treeline, and finally into real forest. This trail is often wet and churned into a morass by moose traffic, but by this time you will be used to wetland walking.

Snug Harbour campsite is at the bottom of the hill. See the trail descriptions for Snug Harbour Trail and Western Brook Pond Trail for the rest of the route out.

Other Backcountry Hiking—Gros Morne offers many off-trail hiking experiences for anyone who is skilled at reading a topographic map and using a compass. You can hike down rivers, across country, up old abandoned trails, along the seacoast, or wherever your sense of adventure leads you. Before attempting any off-trail routes, please speak to Visitor Centre staff for advice. You will require a permit for backcountry camping, and should be aware of travel restrictions within the park's Special Preservation areas. If you take the normal precautions and remember that you alone are responsible for your safety and comfort, you will have a wonderful time exploring the park.

COMMUNITY TRAILS

Some communities have developed short trails that lead to points of interest. All of these are worth exploring, and provide views and experiences that you cannot get elsewhere in the park. Please remember that these trails are not

Short-billed dowitchers, St. Pauls marsh.

Fishing premises, St. Pauls marsh.

necessarily maintained on an annual basis, and can be muddy, somewhat overgrown, and steep in places. Be cautious with handrails, steps, and boardwalks–Newfoundland's climate is not kind to wood.

Cow Head—Cow Head is a limestone peninsula connected by a natural causeway to the community of Cow Head. Maps of the network of trails on the Head are available at the *Tête de Vache Museum* in town. Pond Road will take you to the causeway, and signs on the Head indicate where the trails start. The trails lead to the point of the Head, to the old lighthouse, and onto Big Hill in the centre of the peninsula. Several branches head down to the shore. It is possible to walk completely around the Head on the beach at low tide, but you will have to clamber over rocks and slippery seaweed. Be careful if the wind has raised large waves, since they can be unpredictable. Falling rock is a hazard below the cliffs. Along the way you will see garden plots, the famous Cow Head Conglomerate, wave sculpted rocks, tidepools, tuckamore tangles, and coastal meadows. Cabin development and all-terrain vehicle use are encroaching on this beautiful peninsula—see it while you can.

Norris Point—A trail to the top of Burnt Hill (also known as Big Hill and Neddy's Hill) starts at the end of the road to the left of the Norris Point wharf. The first part is a steep uphill clamber over log steps. The trail then branches in several directions, but the hill is small and easy to explore, and openings in the trees give great views of East Arm, the tilted limestone beds of Shag Cliff, Norris Point, and the Lookout Hills. From the hilltop you can see boats and even whales in the Tickle, and watch the sun set over the bay.

Glenburnie—From a parking area beside the old concrete bridge a very short trail heads upstream to the local swimming hole. Around the corner is a wide waterfall. Be very careful of slippery footing in places.

Trout River—Cross the metal Bailey bridge in the centre of the community. A small sign on the hillside indicates the trail, and a wooden handrail leads uphill from roadside. There are three branches, all with panoramas of the community: Straight ahead is The Old Man, a ten-metre-high sea stack carved during higher sea level 12,000 years ago. Please do not attempt to climb The Old Man, he may be a little unstable. A second trail leads upstream for about one kilometre to a lookoff over Trout River Pond. The third trail heads towards the coast, through a field of wildflowers, into dark tuckamore forest, and out onto a beautiful clifftop meadow atop Western Head.

PARK REGULATIONS

The following are basic national park rules and etiquette. Please remember: while in the park you are responsible for your own safety and for the protection of park resources. By following these rules you will help to ensure your enjoyment of the park, and the safety and enjoyment of others—we ask for your co-operation. If you would like more information, please speak to park staff.

- A national park permit is required by anyone using park facilities from late May to Thanksgiving.
- Hunting is prohibited.
- Guns must be kept unloaded, dismantled, and cased while being transported through the park.
- Freshwater fishing requires a national park license.
- Collecting, damaging, or disturbing plants, animals, antlers, rocks, fossils, human artefacts, or other resources within the park is prohibited.
- Campfires are allowed in designated fireplaces in park campgrounds. Fires are prohibited along trails, hiking routes, and at all backcountry campsites except on the seashore.
- Trail bikes and other vehicles are not allowed on hiking trails. All-terrain vehicles may not be used by park visitors.
- Pets must be leashed at all times within the park. Pets are not allowed on Gros Morne mountain, on park boat tours, or on the Long Range.

READING LIST

Barkham, Selma H. 1989. *The Basque Coast of Newfoundland.* Great Northern Peninsula Development Corporation, Plum Point, Nfld. 24 pp.

Berger, Anthony R. (Co-ordinator), André Bouchard, Ian A. Brookes, Douglas R. Grant, Stuart G. Hay, and Robert K. Stevens. 1992. *Geology, Topography, and Vegetation, Gros Morne National Park, Newfoundland.* Misc. Report 54 pp. Map 1:150,000. Geological Survey of Canada, Ottawa.

Bouchard, André, Stuart G. Hay, Yves Bergeron, and Alain Leduc. 1991. "The Vascular Flora of Gros Morne National Park, Newfoundland: a Habitat Classification Approach Based on Floristic, Biogeographical and Life-form Data." In: *Quantitative Approaches to Phytogeography.* P.L. Nimis and T.J. Covello (Eds.). Kluwer Academic Publishers, The Netherlands. pp. 123-157.

Brookes, Ian A. 1993. "Canadian Landform Examples 26, Table Mountain, Gros Morne National Park, Newfoundland." *The Canadian Geographer* 37:1 69-75.

Burrows, Roger. 1989. *Birding in Atlantic Canada, Newfoundland.* Jesperson Press Ltd., St. John's Nfld. 175 pp.

Burzynski, Michael P., and Anne Marceau. 1990. *Rocks Adrift, the Geology of Gros Morne National Park* (also published as *Le grand voyage des continents, la géologie du parc national du Gros-Morne*). Gros Morne Co-operating Association, Rocky Harbour Nfld. 57 pp.

Brooks, Robert R. 1987. *Serpentine and its Vegetation, a Multidisciplinary Approach.* Dioscorides Press, Portland Oregon. 454 pp.

Caines, Paul, and K. Henrik Deichmann. 1990. *Resource Description and Analysis, Gros Morne National Park.* Internal document, Gros Morne National Park, Rocky Harbour Nfld. 461 pp.

Candow, James E. 1998. *Lomond, The Life and Death of a Newfoundland Woods Town.* Harry Cuff Publications Ltd. St. John's Nfld. 104 pp.

Colman-Sadd, Stephen, and Susan A. Scott. 1994. *Newfoundland & Labrador Traveller's Guide to the Geology.* Nfld. Dept. of Mines and Energy, Geological Survey Branch, St. John's Nfld. Booklet 91 pp., map 1:1,000,000.

Jackson, Douglas (Gerald Penney Ed.). 1993. *"On the Country": the Micmac of Newfoundland.* Harry Cuff Publications Ltd., St. John's Nfld. 172 pp.

James, Noel P. and Robert K. Stevens. 1986. *Stratigraphy and Correlation of the Cambro-Ordovician Cow Head Group, Western Newfoundland.* Bulletin 366, Geological Survey of Canada, Ottawa. 143 pp. plus maps.

McLeod, Pat. 1988. *Gros Morne: A Living Landscape.* Breakwater, St. John's Nfld. 119 pp.

Murphy, Dan, Jim Price, and Kevin Redmond. 1995. *Canyons, Coves & Coastal Waters, Choice Canoe and Kayak Routes of Newfoundland and Labrador.* Breakwater, St. John's Nfld. 143 pp.

Renouf, Priscilla. 1993. "Palaeoeskimo Seal Hunters at Port au Choix Northwestern Newfoundland." In: *Newfoundland Studies.* Vol. 9, No. 2. R.E. Buehler (Ed.). Dept. of

English, MUN, St. John's Nfld. pp. 185-212.

Roberts, Bruce A. 1992. "Ecology of Serpentinized Areas, Newfoundland, Canada." In: *The Ecology of Areas with Serpentinized Rocks. A World* View. B.A. Roberts and J. Proctor (Eds.). Kluwer Academic Publishers, The Netherlands, pp. 75 - 113.

Poole, Cyril F. (Ed.). 1981-1994. *Encyclopedia of Newfoundland and Labrador.* Five vol. Harry Cuff Publications Ltd., St. John's Nfld. 3891 pp.

Rouleau, Ernest, and Gisèle Lamoureux. 1992. *Atlas des plantes vasculaires de l'île de Terre-Neuve et des îles de Saint-Pierre-et-Miquelon; Atlas of the Vascular Plants of the Island of Newfoundland and the Islands of Saint-Pierre-et-Miquelon.* Fleurbec, Saint-Henri-de-Lévis Québec. 777 pp.

Ryan, A. Glen. 1975. *Some Newfoundland Butterflies.* Park Interpretation Publication Number 8, Nfld. Dept. of Environment and Lands, St. John's Nfld. 31 pp.

Ryan, A. Glen. 1978. *Native Trees and Shrubs of Newfoundland and Labrador.* Park Interpretation Publication Number 14, Nfld. Dept. of Environment and Lands, St. John's, Nfld. 120 pp.

South, C. Robin. 1983. *Biogeography and Ecology of the Island of Newfoundland.* Dr. W. Junk Publishers, The Hague. 723 pp.

Story, George M., William J. Kirwin, and John D.A. Widdowson. 1990. *Dictionary of Newfoundland English*, second edition with supplement. University of Toronto Press, Toronto. 770 pp.

Tuck, James A. 1976. *Newfoundland and Labrador Prehistory.* Archaeological Survey of Canada, National Museum of Man, National Museums of Canada, Ottawa. 127 pp.

Tuck, James A. and Robert Grenier. 1989. *Red Bay, Labrador, World Whaling Capital, A.D. 1550-1600.* Atlantic Archaeology Ltd., St. John's Nfld. 68 pp.

TOPOGRAPHIC MAPS

National Topographic System maps of the park area:

12 H/12 Gros Morne, 12 H/13 St. Pauls Inlet, 12 G/9 Skinner Cove, 12 G/8 Trout River, 12 H/5 Lomond, and portions of 12 H/6, 12 H/11, and 12 H/14